Young Writers 2005 POE

Playground Poets
Let your creativity flow...

North West Counties Vol II
Edited by Steve Twelvetree

Young Writers

First published in Great Britain in 2005 by:
Young Writers
Remus House
Coltsfoot Drive
Peterborough
PE2 9JX
Telephone: 01733 890066
Website: www.youngwriters.co.uk

All Rights Reserved

© Copyright Contributors 2005

SB ISBN 1 84602 169 3

Foreword

Young Writers was established in 1991 and has been passionately devoted to the promotion of reading and writing in children and young adults ever since. The quest continues today. Young Writers remains as committed to the fostering of burgeoning poetic and literary talent as ever.

This year's Young Writers competition has proven as vibrant and dynamic as ever and we are delighted to present a showcase of the best poetry from across the UK. Each poem has been carefully selected from a wealth of *Playground Poets* entries before ultimately being published in this, our thirteenth primary school poetry series.

Once again, we have been supremely impressed by the overall high quality of the entries we have received. The imagination, energy and creativity which has gone into each young writer's entry made choosing the best poems a challenging and often difficult but ultimately hugely rewarding task - the general high standard of the work submitted amply vindicating this opportunity to bring their poetry to a larger appreciative audience.

We sincerely hope you are pleased with our final selection and that you will enjoy *Playground Poets North West Counties Vol II* for many years to come.

Contents

Caton Community Primary School, Caton
Lilly Vachon (9)	1
Jack Atkinson (9)	2
Annabelle Holloway (9)	2
Christopher Moorby (10)	3
Sam Dowswell (9)	3
Hannah Woods (10)	4
Katie Burkitt (9)	4
Evie Picton (10)	5
Lawrence Cwerner (9)	6
Nathan Heywood (9)	6
Aaron Mills (9)	6
Sammy Heywood (9)	7
Bethany Walker (8)	7
Alexandra Dickinson (9)	7
Oliver Heywood (9)	8
Kiya Hennefer (9)	8
Lauren Cragg (9)	8
John Longton (9)	9

Cherry Tree Primary School, Lymm
Kate Leather (9)	9
Francesca Young (9)	10
Natalie Davies (9)	10
Elise Barker (8)	11
Charis Stubbs (9)	11
Lily Dyble (8)	12
Jessica Hine (7)	12
Ellie Coughlan (9)	13
Anam Ijaaz (8)	13
Duncan Hughes (8)	14
Edward Bennett (9)	14
Thomas May (10)	15
Emily Copland (10)	15
Helen McLaughlin (7)	16
Eleanor Baillie (7)	16
Georgina Watkins (8)	17
Laura McKenzie (7)	17
Connor Sheron (8)	18

Joseph Waters (7) 18
Ella Wyss (8) 18
Laura Fitzgibbon (10) 19
Patrick Mottershead (10) 19
Harry Evans (9) 20
Alice Selwood (8) 20

Eccleston CE Primary School, Chester
Sarah Elsley (10) 21
Robert Bowler (9) 21
Matthew Johnson (10) 22
Leah Morley (10) 23
Grace McDermott (10) 24
Chloé Jones (9) 24
Juliana Hatwell (11) 25
Josh Davies (9) 25
Josh Horrocks (10) 26
James Bowler (7) 26
Rebekah Kelly (9) 27
Holly Shaw (9) 27
Skye Paul (10) 27
Anna Fearnall (10) 28
Grace Rowland (9) 28
Polly Mackarel (10) 29
Alexander Thomas (8) 29
Jenny Tilston (8) 30
Rhys Williams (10) 30
Henry Makings (8) 31
Matthew Booth (8) 31
Portia Kitney (8) 32
Megan Gittings (9) 32
James Baker (9) 33
Samuel Squires (7) 33
Andrew Bolton (7) 33
Lucy Fearnall (8) 34
Luke Faulkner (8) 34
Lauren Ellis (7) 34
Hari Griffith (7) 35
James Austin (9) 35
Rowan Stuart (7) 35
Katy Evans (8) 36

Lily Bissell (8)	36
Nelson Hughes (9)	36
Luke Rowland (7)	37
Thomas Rose (8)	37
Edward Adams (7)	37
Calum West (10)	38
Jamie Handley (9)	38
Timothy Tipping (8)	38

Marsden CP School, Nelson

Isaaq Mohammed (11)	39
Ummeya Zaka (9)	40
Bethany Owen (9)	41
Misbah J Ali (9)	41
Zeshan Mahmood (9)	42
Aqil Javed (8)	42
Sayra Gillani (9)	43

Marsh Green Primary School, Wigan

Jade Sherman (10)	43
Natalie Hewitt (11)	44
David Glynn	44

Mossley CE (VC) Primary School, Congleton

Danielle Searle (9)	45
Louise Walley (10)	45
Alice Jones (8)	46
Aaron Nuttall (9)	47
George Harper (8)	47
Hollie Kiely (8)	48
Ellis Frodsham (9)	48
Adam Ball (8)	49
John Evans (8)	49
Jordan Grocott (8)	50
James Ball (9)	51
Emma Roxburgh (7)	52
Kyle McLellan (8)	53
Danielle Tatton (8)	54
Rebecca Jackson (8)	55
Megan Hogg (8)	56

Luke Harpur (8)	57
Lauren Myatt (8)	58
Andrew Kruze (8)	59
Hannah Johnson (7)	60
Thomas Derbyshire (9)	61
Charlotte Oakley (8)	61
Kimberley Wilson (7)	62
Isaac Pemberton (9)	62
Daniel Loach (9)	63

Murdishaw West Community Primary School, Runcorn

Leah Carney (8)	63
Jordan Stoba (9)	64
Luke Reddington (8)	64
Regan Jolliffe (8)	65
Samantha Kneale (9)	65
James Ward (8)	66
Lewis Hughes (9)	66
Gemma Lenahan (8)	67
Alisha Parker (9)	67

Overleigh St Mary's Primary School, Chester

Rachel Tompkins (8)	68
Amy Bebbington (8)	68
Freya Brewis (9)	69
Seren Challand (8)	69
Anna Houghton (9)	70
Amber Houlders (9)	70
David Cavendish (9)	71
James McDermott (8)	71
Sophie Wilkin (10)	72
Joseph Speed (8)	72
Merika Holmes (11)	73
Hannah Aird (8)	73
Louise Tompkins (10)	74
Amy Lawrence (8)	74
Peter O'Donoghue (8)	75
Jenny Thomas (9)	75
Jennifer Williams (8)	76
Lucy Powell (9)	76
Elizabeth Cousins (8)	77

Esther Maiden (8)	77
Lily Wearden (8)	78
Kathryn Cowley (8)	78
Jade Robson (11)	79
Leah Newell	79
Callum Boyd (9)	80
Sumera Sharif (7)	80
Anna L Grainger (10)	81
Isabella Brown (8)	81
Abbey Badaei (11)	82
Samuel Davies (8)	82
Alice Johnson (7)	83
Amelia Jones (8)	83
Ben Preston (10)	84
Jasmine Blythin (10)	84
Adam Kassab (11)	85
Isaac Jones (10)	85
Lily Walton (11)	86
Douglas Kent (10)	86
Hannah Lord (11)	87
Amy Landsborough (10)	87
Alex Halliwell-Dykes (8)	88
Matthew Harle (11)	88
Daisy A Speed (9)	89
Flora McWilliam (9)	89
Sophie Powell (11)	90
Rhiannon Owen (7)	90
Alec Shuttleworth (10)	90
Danny Ward (10)	91
Adam Thomson (8)	91
Megan Kelly (9)	92
Aoife Doyle (10)	92
Sam Ellams (10)	92
Charlotte Ninnes (10)	93
Jeremy Telford (9)	93
Samuel Garratt (9)	93
Beth Hallam (9)	94
Louise Evans (8)	94
Alice Byrne (9)	94
Stephanie Reay (8)	95
Georgia Bundy (8)	95
Demi Chelsea Tsimbilakis (9)	95

Sophie Witherstone (9)	96
Richard Grainger (10)	96
Ned Pitt Knowles (9)	96
Rachael Alcock (9)	97
Jack Watson (10)	97
Olivia Johnston (9)	98
Kirsty Stubbert (9)	98
Sean Telford (9)	99
Tom Inns (9)	99
Lewis Smith (8)	100
Isaac Scott (9)	100
Luke Goldsmith (8)	101
Alexander Benson (8)	101
Anna Brodie (8)	102
Joel Langmead (8)	102
Joy Hunter (7)	103
Ceri Chase (8)	103
Olivia Brett (8)	104
Sophie Ferguson (9)	104
Duncan Ritchie (8)	105
Joseph Hannigan (9)	105
Alexandra McNee (9)	106
Sean Schooling (10)	106
Jake Brandon Venables (9)	107
Jordan Chellig (7)	107
Samuel Hale (9)	108
Holly Pitt Knowles (8)	108
Ben Gregory (7)	109
Niall Rogers (8)	109
Alice Rees (7)	110
Olivia Gough	110
Molly Jones (8)	111
Sarah Thomas (10)	111
Michael Cavendish (9)	112
William Watson (7)	112
Rhys Williams (9)	113
Niamh Doyle (7)	113
Emma Jones (8)	114
Charles Tice (7)	114
Melissa Jones (8)	115
Lucy Clegg (8)	115
Meg Rawlinson (10)	116

Callum Gough (7) 116
Mary Scott (11) 117
Tom Batten (9) 117
Christopher McCartney (7) 118
Mollie McIlwaine (7) 118
Harry Redmayne (9) 118
Peter Young (11) 119
Jake Parry (9) 119
Molly Degg (8) 119

St James' CE School, Clitheroe
Chris Ratcliffe (10) 120
Victoria Jackson (8) 120
Emma Hook (11) 121
Linda Sou (8) 121
Lauren Ross (8) 121
Jodi Novak (11) 122
Kirby Robinson (9) 122
Zoë Clayton (10) 123
Mark Faulkner (8) 123
Lauren Barton (10) 124
Natasha Watson (9) 124
Jake Nuttall (10) 125
Jack Dewhurst (8) 125
Ellie Tolson (10) 126
Joshua Mansfield (10) 126
Katie Moss (9) 127
Charli Charnley (9) 127
Jack Knowles (10) 128
Luke Gregson (9) 128
Rebecca Dixon (11) 129
Liam Nuttall (11) 129
Bethany Tomlinson (11) 130
Jake Place (9) 130
Robert Hembury (9) 130
Victoria Rose (8) 131
Aimee Neild (8) 131
Shannon Braithwaite (9) 131
Jessamy Britcliffe (7) 132
Kirsten Hunt (8) 132
Jordan Rose (11) 133

Jack Ryan (7)	133
Natalie Bristol (8)	133
Laura-Jane O'Neil (11)	134
Emily Aspinall (10)	134
Sarah Anne Margaret Davies (11)	135
Christopher O'Reilly (10)	135
Tyler Spencer (11)	136
Reece Monk (7)	136
Jeremy Piercy (10)	136
Ben Rose (11)	137
Poppy Johns (10)	137
Melissa Cox (9)	137
Adam Johnson (10)	138
Wesleigh Russell (11)	138
Amber Townley (10)	139
Lindsay Roberts (11)	139
Tom McBride (11)	139
Naomi White (10)	140
Matthew Johnston (7)	140
Aron Stevenson (9)	140
Henri Webber (10)	141
Levi Barnes (7)	141
Paige Bithell (7)	141
Sam Townsend (11)	142
Ilona-Jade Worsley (9)	142
Amber Barnes (7)	142
Paul Coward (11)	143
Rhian Melvin (9)	143
Cian Lee (9)	143
Helen Sou (9)	144
Hannah Marshall (10)	144
Billie-Jo Jackson (11)	145
Emma Fosberry (8)	145
Dean Gordon (10)	146

St John's CEP School, Nelson

Callum Dickinson (9)	146
Philippa Dinsdale (9)	147
Scarlett Kinsella (9)	147
Luke Parkinson (9)	148
Usman Arif (9)	148

Aaron Hirst (10)	149
Anthony Denney (9)	149
Richard Bailey (9)	150
Katherine Illingworth (9)	150

St Thomas' CE Primary School, Leigh

Lauren Atherton (10)	151
Laura Mulcahy (9)	151
Bethany Cook (10)	152
Phillip Whitehead (10)	153
Callum Leyland (10)	153
Rebecca Healey (9)	154
Kelliejo Colbert (9)	154
Matthew Lambert (11)	155
Lauren English-Rowland (9)	155
Heather Morris (9)	155
Sam Rowlands (10)	156
Rayyah Unsworth (9)	156
Paige Briscoe (9)	156
Helen Slater (10)	157
Kirstin Houghton (9)	157
Chloé Yates (9)	158
Lucy Mellan (10)	158
Ashley Pritchard (9)	159
Heather Garfin (9)	159
Jessica Bridget Anderson (11)	160
Amy Boardman (9)	160
Stephanie Boardman (10)	161
Abigail O'Brien (9)	161
Gemma Stockley (10)	162
Simon Lowe (9)	163
Shelby Harris (9)	163
Adam Wilkes (10)	164
Craig Town (9)	165
Anna Woodburn (9)	165
Hope Gill-Daintith (10)	166
Paul Burke (10)	166
Clare Aikin (8)	167
Jack Morris (9)	167
Amy Knowles (8)	168
McCauley Collier (8)	168

Darren Jackson (9)	169
Lisa Billington (11)	169
Lewis Birkbeck (8)	170
Bethany Taylor (10)	170
Joanna Morris (8)	171
Rebecca Brighton (10)	171
Ruby Taylor (8)	172
Zack Uzokwe (8)	173
Jodie Kniveton (10)	173
Jessica Unsworth (8)	174
James Stuart Massey (9)	174
Lauren Oakes (10)	175
Ashley Pavitt (9)	175
Adam Williams (11)	176
Bayley Swinburn (9)	176
Sam Boydell (10)	177
Paul Turner (9)	177
Rebecca Lowe (11)	178
Jamie Taylor (9)	178
Jessica Mathews (11)	179
Jenny Goodison (11)	179
Natalie Hilton (10)	180
Jack Castledine (10)	181
Jemma Bentham (8)	181
Anthony Smith (10)	182
Sylvia Clayton (11)	182
Jenna Stevenson (11)	183
Matthew Naughton (11)	183
Lucy Taberner (9)	184
Emma Taberner (8)	185
Molly Newport (9)	185
Abbie Cox (7)	186
Matthew Taylor (7)	186
Harry Thompson (8)	186
Katie Unsworth (8)	187
James Pickles (7)	187
Kirsty Anderton (9)	187
Jilly Westhead (7)	188
Adam Oakes (7)	188
Katie Hickson (7)	188
Leah Burke (8)	189
Bethany Sharrock (7)	189

Lauren Smith (9)	189
Siobhan Ryan (10)	190
Bethany Robinson (10)	191
Marnie Bickett (9)	191
Jennel Anne Kalyan Unsworth (10)	192
Emma Kennerly (11)	193
Alison Meeson (10)	193
Jessica Marsh (9)	194
Catherine Buckley (10)	194
Kerry Linley (9)	195
Nicole Pendlebury (10)	195

Shavington Primary School, Crewe

Paige Mary-Louise Jackson (10)	196
Jessica Lea Youle (11)	196
Hope Kurzawa (10)	197
Jamie Millington (11)	197
Francesca Wilkinson (11)	198
Lydia Oakley (10)	198
Olivia Jackson (11)	199
Daniel Simon (10)	199
Laura Vickers (11)	200
Tom Atkinson (10)	200
Amy Howes (10)	201
Rebecca Fearnley (10)	201
Lloyd Phillips (10)	202
Rebecca Prince (10)	202
Glenn Muirhead (11)	203

Woodfield Primary School, Chester

Jamie Flynn (11)	203
Georgia Bailiff (11)	204
Mia Gatward (11)	204
Ben Pace (10)	205
Ryan Smith (11)	205
William Gunning (11)	206
Evan McKinney (10)	206
Alice Ankers (10)	207
Dale Williams (11)	207
Hasna Begum Ali (11)	208
Sabir Kader (10)	208

Floyd Williams (10)	209
George Welsh (10)	209
Lewis Whitehouse (11)	210
Abbie Hallmark (10)	210
Jennifer Plank (11)	211
Andrew Leigh (11)	211

The Poems

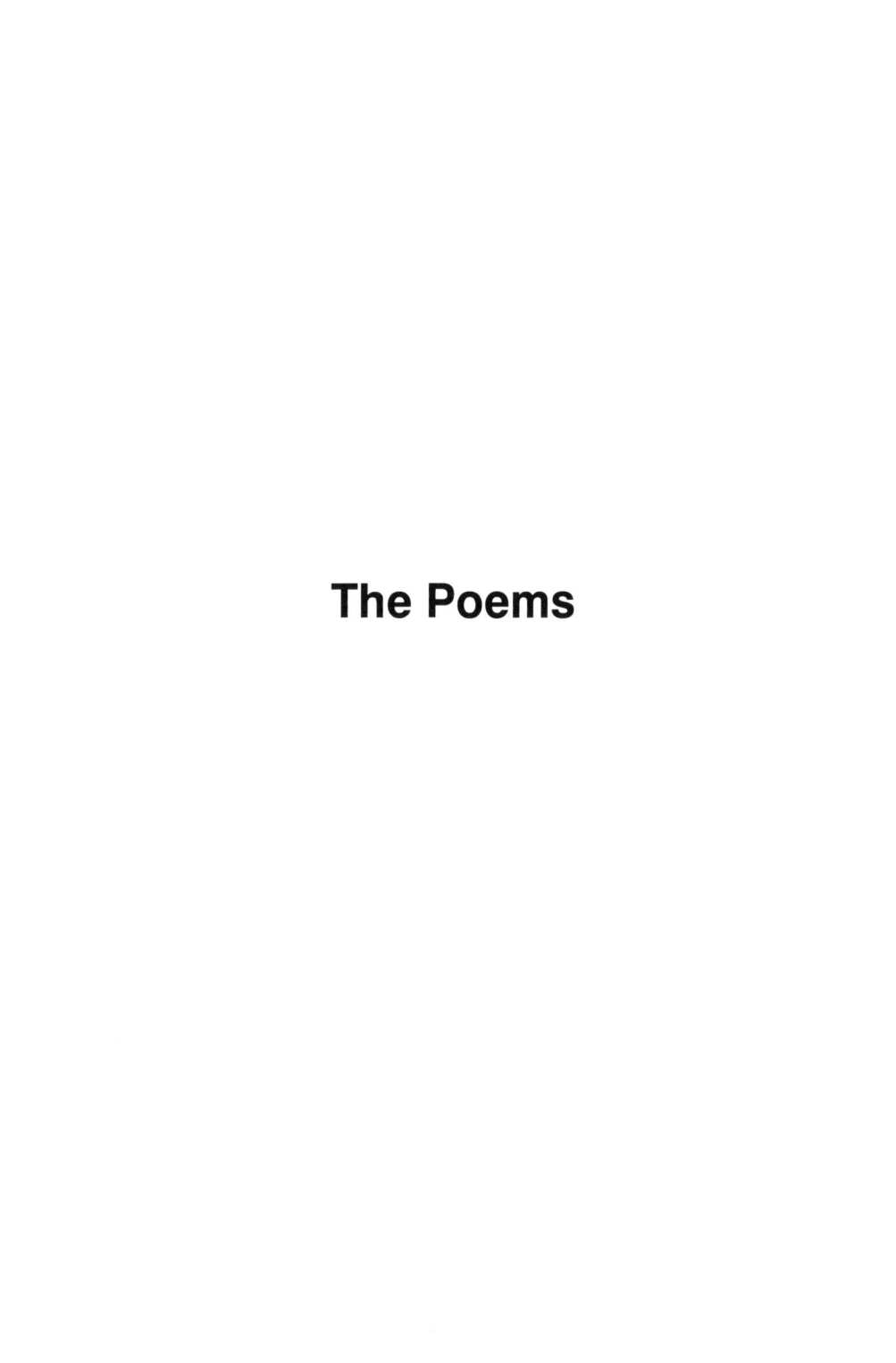

Spring

Trees

I like it when trees start growing buds,
On their fingertip twigs all bony.
I like it when trees start growing blossom,
From white, pink and yellow to petals and leaves.
I like it when trees give a cheery wave,
In the mist and the rain and the breezy wind.

Flowers

I like the flowers that are pink, yellow, red,
The ones that smell different from the others.
I like the flowers that are pretty and elegant,
I like the ones that are scary and big.
I like flowers, all kinds from A-Z.

Seeds

I like the seeds that are round and plump,
I like the seeds that are thin and long,
The seeds I like best, though, are the
Ones that are spotty and smooth!
It's the seeds that are odd
And different that are the best.

Friends

My friends are the thing I like best.
When you wake up in the morning,
You call for someone to say hello,
Set off for school and be happy.
Friends are always there for you,
All through the year!

Lilly Vachon (9)
Caton Community Primary School, Caton

The Great Fire Of London

I can see devastated people without homes,
Grey smoke spreading from house to house.
Red, yellow and orange flames spreading
From house to house high out of my sight,
And flailing arms whacking other people and buildings.

I feel beaten by horror, really, really beaten,
Sadness flows into me like water in a cup.
I feel terrified of being killed by the fire,
I feel any minute now I'm going to burst into tears like a baby.

I can hear babies wailing in the background,
People are screaming and running away from the fire.
I can hear houses creaking and falling down,
Flames are crackling and burning hard.

Jack Atkinson (9)
Caton Community Primary School, Caton

Laughter

Laughter can be
bright red and can
be dark.
It sounds
like a whistle in
the distance.
It tastes like a
liquorice stick.
It smells like
lavender in the air.
It looks like bright
and dark colours.
It feels like a ball.
It reminds me of fun.

Annabelle Holloway (9)
Caton Community Primary School, Caton

Silence

Silence is black and white
like night-time with stars sparkling,
it's like a haunted mansion
and like creaky, creaky stairs.
Silence tastes like air curling around the room
and twisters coming towards you.
Silence smells of emptiness
like nothing is around you.
Silence looks like a ghost is around you.
Silence feels like loneliness
and scared bats are flapping around you.
Silence reminds you of someone
who has died at midnight.

Christopher Moorby (10)
Caton Community Primary School, Caton

Annoyed

Annoyed reminds me of brothers teasing me,
When I do a good picture, they screw it up.
Annoyed is dark red and dark black,
Annoyed is like somebody killing your pet,
Annoyed sounds like somebody drumming like mad in your ear,
Annoyed is burnt sausages in your kitchen,
Annoyed tastes like expensive Asda's mouldy beef,
Annoyed feels like anger going in your blood,
Annoyed looks like thunder setting your house on *fire*.

Sam Dowswell (9)
Caton Community Primary School, Caton

Sometimes I Wonder

There are some things I haven't understood,
Throughout all my life,
Like, why use a fork
And why use a knife?
And why wear shoes
And not walk around barefoot?
And why make a door
Open and shut?

Sometimes I wonder
About all of these things,
And sometimes I wonder
What the future brings.
But maybe I should just wait and see
What my life has laid out for me.

I sometimes wonder
How other people feel,
And sometimes I wonder
If what I see is real,
'Cause sometimes I see
A flicker in the corner of my eye,
But when I look up
Into the sky,
There is nothing to be seen.

Hannah Woods (10)
Caton Community Primary School, Caton

Evil

Evil is a fiery red when your carpet catches light,
Evil sounds like a dinosaur's roar,
Evil tastes like mouldy cheese and moss,
Evil smells like slurry out of a green field,
Evil looks like lava erupting out of a volcano,
Evil feels like falling in glowing green toxic waste,
Evil reminds me of the teeth of a shark.

Katie Burkitt (9)
Caton Community Primary School, Caton

Babies

Soft skin,
Smelly bums,
So cute,
Love their mums.

They always sleep,
Sometimes weep,
Safe and sound,
They'll rouse around,
They like to play,
They are mini sunshine rays.

Soft skin,
Smelly bums,
So cute,
Love their mums.

They love a cuddle,
Sometimes in a muddle,
The cheeky monkeys
Get teeth that are chunky,
Button noses
That smell like pink roses.

Soft skin,
Smelly bums,
So cute,
Love their mums.

Everyone has to like babies!

Evie Picton (10)
Caton Community Primary School, Caton

Horrify

Horrify is as black as a moonless night,
Horrify sounds like someone being tortured,
Horrify tastes like worms in fresh soil,
Horrify smells like people who never wash,
Horrify looks like something you can't imagine,
Horrify feels like a poisonous spider sinking its fangs into my skin,
Horrify reminds me of my worst nightmares.

Lawrence Cwerner (9)
Caton Community Primary School, Caton

Stress

Stress is dark red like splashes of blood,
It sounds like a train's whistle,
It tastes like a spider on your tongue,
It smells like burning fire on your head,
It looks like a demon,
It feels hot and boiling,
it reminds me of anger and fear.

Nathan Heywood (9)
Caton Community Primary School, Caton

Hate

Hate is like a ball of fire,
It sounds like a bullet shooting out of a gun,
It feels like your teeth grinding, like a brick scraping
Against a metal fence,
You can feel the flames in your eyes, hurting your eyes.

Aaron Mills (9)
Caton Community Primary School, Caton

Coldness

The cold is blue like frozen water,
It whistles like my school playground whistle,
It tastes like water in my freezer,
It smells like minty toothpaste,
It looks like the colour of ice,
It feels like snow falling from the sky,
It reminds me of winter.

Sammy Heywood (9)
Caton Community Primary School, Caton

Happiness

Happiness is silver like my dog's collar,
   It makes a soft sound,
      It's like a butterfly on your tongue,
         It smells like fresh air.
            It looks like a rainbow,
               It feels like butterflies in your tummy,
                  It reminds me of summer.

Bethany Walker (8)
Caton Community Primary School, Caton

Love

Love is warm, pink and red, it sounds like birds in a flower bed,
It taste like strawberries, nice and smooth,
It smells like flowers on the move,
It looks like a heart moving all around,
It feels smoothe but no sound.
It reminds me of beaches, running round and round.

Alexandra Dickinson (9)
Caton Community Primary School, Caton

Darkness

Darkness is like black with no light shining,
It's no noise at all,
It tastes like hailstones,
It smells like thunder and lightning,
It looks like rain,
It feels like raindrops,
It reminds me of Hogwarts Express.

Oliver Heywood (9)
Caton Community Primary School, Caton

Excitement

Excitement is pink like roses
It sounds like bells tinkling
It tastes like sweet strawberries
It looks like stars twinkling.
Excitement smells like fresh autumn rain
It feels like bubbles popping and fizzing inside you
It reminds me of my birthday.

Kiya Hennefer (9)
Caton Community Primary School, Caton

Love

Love is pink,
it sounds like fluttering in the sky,
it tastes like fresh picked strawberries,
it smells like lovely candles,
it looks like a big love heart,
it feels like my silky pyjamas,
it reminds me of my mum and dad.

Lauren Cragg (9)
Caton Community Primary School, Caton

Digger

Diggers are good, yellow and blue,
Orange and red, me and you,
They have flashing lights, bright orange,
Nice, lovely, tidy cabs or muddy, ruined and horrible.
They make a noise like a jazzing sound
Your buttons and switches are too fiddly
So many wires tucked away
I like them like that and that is that.

John Longton (9)
Caton Community Primary School, Caton

My Brother's A Monster

My brother's a monster
I want you to know
My brother's a monster
His brain is as tiny as his little toe!

My brother's a monster
He tugs at my hair
My brother's a monster
He threw the sofa right down the stairs!

My brother's a monster
He smashed all the mugs
My brother's a monster
He even eats bugs!

My brother's a monster
No, he really won't share
My brother's a monster
My family don't care!

Kate Leather (9)
Cherry Tree Primary School, Lymm

Winter Feather

The winter feather went away
And back and forwards nearly every day.
It spun around and fell on the ground
And made a lovely winter sound,
Crickle, crickle, crack, crack.
The winter feather flew up and fell on my back
Flutter, flutter, fly away
We'll come back soon on another day
As we fly up right into the sky
We see all the streets and houses below
Then it will really, really start to snow.
Feeling all the cold air blowing in your face,
Sometimes you've got to say to yourself, get on your case,
As I look down at the lovely view I say to myself,
Am I dreaming, is this true?
Winter feather's drifting away and says it will come back in May
I feel sad, but I know that I will see it another day.

Francesca Young (9)
Cherry Tree Primary School, Lymm

My Family!

My sister's a vampire, she sucks my blood
My sister's a vampire, I know she would.
My mum's a mummy, she spooks my dreams
My mum's a mummy, she says I'm in my teens.
My dad's a devil, he does all the chores
My dad's a devil, he has long, pointy claws.
My brother's a burglar, he takes my ted
My brother's a burglar, he took my bed.
Me and my sister, well we're just us
We don't really care, we don't make a *fuss!*

Natalie Davies (9)
Cherry Tree Primary School, Lymm

A German Pilot

What can you see?
White horse waves pushing against the rocks on the English Channel,
White, tall, long cliffs of Dover.
What can you hear?
The petrol working its way through the engine,
The noise of bullets shouting up at you
A plane explosion in front of you.
What can you feel?
The vibration of the rocky nose plane,
The air blowing into your face.
What can you smell?
Frightening bullets coming towards you,
The smell of fear.

Elise Barker (8)
Cherry Tree Primary School, Lymm

My Gran

My gran is as special as a star
Her hair is like a bouncy balloon
Her eyes are like a brown bear
Her face is like the shining sun.
When she walks she is like a queen
When she sits she is like a teddy bear
When she laughs she is like a bird singing
When she sleeps she is very peaceful.
The best thing about my gran
Is she is always kind and never mean!

Charis Stubbs (9)
Cherry Tree Primary School, Lymm

Setting Off

What can you see?
I see my mum waving to me as the train sets off
I see mums crying to see us go, children waving to their mums
Some are glad to go, I see my mum running with the train
Trying to get one more look at me.
What can you hear?
I can hear children crying, some howling,
The clink of the train grumbling along the track,
Teacher's failing to keep us quiet, people singing to keep spirits bright.
What can you feel?
I can feel tears coming to my eyes
My mum's arms around me, her sweet voice calling my name
I feel her arm on my shoulder, I feel my heart sink.
What can you smell?
I can smell my mum, my sweet bed in my empty room,
The smell of bombs dropping.

Lily Dyble (8)
Cherry Tree Primary School, Lymm

Sad Evacuee

What can you see?
The train shining in the sun,
The steam misting in the air.
What can you hear?
The engine of the train,
The shout of the other children.
What can you feel?
Your bag as heavy as an elephant,
Other people hitting you with hard bags.
What can you smell?
The smell of diesel from the train
Bread from the baker's.

Jessica Hine (7)
Cherry Tree Primary School, Lymm

The Magic Eagle

Eagle flying, passing by
In the summer moonlit sky.
His wings will shimmer in the light
Never stopping in his flight.

Some day people here will see,
This eagle is very magic and free.
He can easily catch his prey,
Getting mice from day to day.

You can see magic in his wings
And beak, feathers, eyes and things.
But never lasts a day without,
Sleeping, feeding and having a pout.

It's nearly sunset, the eagle finds,
The magic slowly combines!

Ellie Coughlan (9)
Cherry Tree Primary School, Lymm

Tutankhamen Discovered

Howard Carter found the tomb
Of the ancient Tutankhamen
His foreman Ali found the step
But Howard Carter did the rest
It was the secret wall he knocked right down
Though Caenarvon thinks he's a clown
There it was lying there
Tutankhamen with hardly any hair.
'I found it, I found it,' he suddenly cried
After that Lord Carnarvon sadly died.
Howard Carter was so proud
He shouted and screamed ever so loud
It was famous he became
All the other archaeologists wanted the same.

Anam Ijaaz (8)
Cherry Tree Primary School, Lymm

Army Tanks

What can you see?
Bullets flying through the air
Army tanks all around me shooting at the Germans
Bullets flying at me
The German army marching at me with their guns over their shoulders
Some Germans shooting and others ready to shoot
I am swerving in and out of them.

What can you hear?
Exploding bombs here and there
The sound of German bombs flying overhead
Army tanks rumbling on the stones
The yelling of injured soldiers.

What can you feel?
The rumbling of the bottom of my tank
A vibration in my wheel.

What can you smell?
Lots and lots of smoke and the smell of fear.

Duncan Hughes (8)
Cherry Tree Primary School, Lymm

The Hardship Of War

War is wrong, peace is right,
The skulls that break in the night.
I feel pain that you cannot
Because of fear of being shot.
I lie here solemn as stone
I lie here with a broken bone.
It's the end of time
As I leave, I leave my crimes.
I hear the cries in my head
I lie here, still and dead.

Edward Bennett (9)
Cherry Tree Primary School, Lymm

Weapons

Shields can be blue
Shields can be red
They can be funny colours
When I am thinking of them in my head
Swords can be yellow
Swords can be green
When they're against you
They can be very, very mean
Bows can be brown
Bows can be gold
When they're left in the snow
They can be very cold
Spears can be white
Spears can be black
They can hurt very much
When they stab you in the back.

Thomas May (10)
Cherry Tree Primary School, Lymm

My Favourite Meal

Spaghetti and marshmallows
With ketchup on the top
Melted chocolate on the side
Washed down with fizzy pop!

Cake mix splodged with sweeties
Pancakes with lemon juice
Sticky toffee pudding
Dragged down with chocolate mousse!

Curry with cheese pizza
Chips and boneless fish
Apple pie with sugar
Served on a silver dish!

Emily Copland (10)
Cherry Tree Primary School, Lymm

The Evacuee

What can you see?
The city moving away from the train
My mum waving, waving with tears in her eyes
Children with labels on them.
What can you hear?
Children crying about leaving home
The train chugging along.
What can you feel?
My heart pounding as I wonder what it'll be like
The cold air blowing against me.
What can you smell?
The smells of animals I've never seen before
The smell of food cooking.

Helen McLaughlin (7)
Cherry Tree Primary School, Lymm

Untitled

What can you see?
I can see cuts, bruises and ill people and people being sick.
What can you hear?
Lots of coughing, snoring and blood dripping.
What can you feel?
I can feel my hat and my tight uniform.
What can you smell?
A horrible damp smell.

Eleanor Baillie (7)
Cherry Tree Primary School, Lymm

Evacuee

What can you see?
Strangers taking children,
People getting pushed to get someone to take them.
What can you hear?
The chugging of the train,
Stomping shoes on the floor, the crunching into the apple.
What can you feel?
My safety pin spiking and pricking against me
My suitcase and gas mask box whacking against me.
What can you smell?
The people who have been munching the apples
Are smelling of apples and pears
The adults' aftershave and perfume.

Georgina Watkins (8)
Cherry Tree Primary School, Lymm

The Sad Evacuee

What can you see?
A train with lots of other children on it
And mums and dads crying into their hankies.
What can you hear?
Children saying goodbye to their mums and dads
Or whoever's taking them.
What can you feel?
The pin on the label scratching me.
What can you smell?
The steam puffing out the train.

Laura McKenzie (7)
Cherry Tree Primary School, Lymm

Armed Bombers

What can you see?
Cities being destroyed by bombs falling from the sky,
Explosions falling every second ploughing the ground.

What can you hear?
Bullets crashing against the plane, bangs banging everywhere
Explosions from the enemy planes.

What can you feel?
Hot air blowing across my face
Buttons being pressed down to let the bombs go off.

What can you smell?
Oil keeping the engine running, the smell of anger.

Connor Sheron (8)
Cherry Tree Primary School, Lymm

Flying In The Air

What can you see?
You can see the Luftwaffe trying to shoot you down
You can see the bullets.
What can you hear?
You can hear the rumbling
You can hear the bullets firing out of the planes.
What can you feel?
You can feel your steering wheel trembling.

Joseph Waters (7)
Cherry Tree Primary School, Lymm

My Fish

My fish can ride a bicycle
My fish can climb a tree
My fish is not like other fish
My fish can't swim like me.

Ella Wyss (8)
Cherry Tree Primary School, Lymm

Different People

Fat, podgy, splodgy and round
Thin, slim, skinny and tall
Lean, mean, nasty and horrid
Sweet, gentle, happy and small.

English, African and American
Chinese, Indian as well
Spanish, French and Swedish
We're all the same.

Blonde, grey, ginger and brown
Brunette, black and white hair
Blue, brown, hazel and green
Grey and dark brown eyes.

We are all the same in different ways
Inside is what you should see
Our looks and abilities do not matter
You can be friends.

Laura Fitzgibbon (10)
Cherry Tree Primary School, Lymm

War

War is bloody,
War is scary,
War is evil
And it makes you scream.
Planes going,
Planes spinning,
Planes shooting all around
In comes the army
And bombs going barmy
Boom goes a tank once more.

Patrick Mottershead (10)
Cherry Tree Primary School, Lymm

My Grandma Poem!

My gran is as kind as a big softie
Her hair is like a grey ball
And the other grandma's hair is as brown as bark.
Her eyes are like brown and green leaves
And her face is like a smiling circle, like a wrinkly old chatterbox.
When she walks she is like a busy slowcoach
When she sits she is like a lazy bird that cuddles everybody.
When she laughs she is like a very funny hyena
When she sleeps she is like a loud snoring speaker
The best thing about my grandma is she loves me
And lets me have loads of sweets, peanuts, flapjacks,
Biscuits, chocolates, cakes, ice cream and mints
And spoils me like a small, cheeky monkey.

Harry Evans (9)
Cherry Tree Primary School, Lymm

Me As An Evacuee

What can you see?
A train full of children and strangers
I see lots of animals on the way and while I'm there
I see very mean people's houses that look scary from the outside.
What can you hear?
A touch of a bang in my ear
The German planes just above.
What can you feel?
I feel Dad is alright
I might just drop all of my things.
What can you smell?
I smell all of the animals at the farm and lovely fresh bread.

Alice Selwood (8)
Cherry Tree Primary School, Lymm

Horse And Rider

Horses are elegant creatures,
Each one as delicate as glass,
Their coats shimmer in the sunlight,
They neigh gracefully as you pass.

Then the rider mounts the horse
And slowly goes to walk,
Out of the blue the horse starts to neigh
As if he's trying to talk.

As the horses parade around the arena,
Listen out for their thundering hooves,
As they move around the arena floor,
They carefully show off their moves.

Once the horse gets very tired
The rider dismounts the steed,
The horse is very hungry,
He's ready for his evening feed.

Sarah Elsley (10)
Eccleston CE Primary School, Chester

The Upset

The football season has arrived
The players clean their boots with pride
The coach talks tactics in the dressing room
They will invade the pitch quite soon

The opposition quake with fear
As giant killing reds appear
A coin is tossed, the whistle blown
Will it be away or home?

Surprise, surprise, the home team scores
Supporters stand and wave and roar
It happens time and time again
The reds, defeated, walk in shame.

Robert Bowler (9)
Eccleston CE Primary School, Chester

The School's Seasons

In spring I walk on the playground
And hear school bells ring.
Back again, here for school
Even though there's no swimming pool.
Starting lessons such as maths
Then get out your pens, you're on the right path.
Then we do our history lesson
Henry VIII makes a wonderful impression
Then we have a go at art
We get out our pencils and make a start.

In summer I walk on the grass
Wondering if I'd be learning outside with the rest of the class
Sometimes it gets really hot
We must work hard to find a cool spot
No air-conditioning to keep us cool
I wish we had a swimming pool.

In autumn I look outside
The wind blows with or without pride
I look at a tree
It is half-past three.
I want to go and play
It is the end of the day
I run onto the playground
Hoping I could ask my mate round
I begin to rise, I'm a bit surprised
With a blow of the wind I have a good spin
I can't believe my eyes.

In winter I walk on the snow
Knowing something everyone else would know
It's nearly Christmas and Santa's on his way
All we have to do now is a nativity play.
Decorations in the hall
Somebody thought it was the mall
Tinsel swaying on the tree,
People singing, 'Deck the halls with boughs of holly'
We're all kept inside so we don't get wet
We're watching a movie, so I've gotta jet.

Matthew Johnson (10)
Eccleston CE Primary School, Chester

The Last Unicorn

A unicorn
Sparkles in the moonlight
Dances in the lake
Mare as white as snow.

A cry from a distance
Soon awakens her from a dream
A cry as a warning
That death is here and run.

Her feet soon pick up
And start to race like mad
Her friends soon join in
And one by one they fall.

She is all alone now
No unicorn alive around her
No horns in their heads
And are now covered in blood.

A sudden shot alarms her
As she started to leap away
Pain suddenly strikes her
Her mouth drips with blood.

Slowly she falls
As she grows weaker and weaker
But she knows one thing
As her head hits the ground.

Leah Morley (10)
Eccleston CE Primary School, Chester

Wolf

Wood stalker
Midnight walker
Sunrise sleeper
Animal eater
Piercing eyes
Silently lies
Forest creeper
Moonlight sneaker
Vicious fighter
Fearsome biter
Shrill howler
Deep growler
Catches prey
Every day
Gives us a scare
Here and there.

Grace McDermott (10)
Eccleston CE Primary School, Chester

Cats

My cat's name is Alfie,
He is only small,
He eats a lot every week,
He loves jumping up the wall.
My cat likes going outside,
He always miaows at the door,
I always have to feed him,
But then it goes all over the floor.

Chloé Jones (9)
Eccleston CE Primary School, Chester

Alfie

A little grey bundle
Dumped as a puppy
No name, no collar, no home.

With his bright, black eyes
He spied a young lady
Tidying her car.

He bounded around her vehicle
As she sped along the roadway
And went to stay with men in blue
Who said, 'We really can't keep you.'

A kindly old lady heard about him
And there he resides with four feline friends
So all is well with him now!

Juliana Hatwell (11)
Eccleston CE Primary School, Chester

I'd Love A Pet Spider

I'd love a pet spider
But Mum said, 'No.

You have a dog, a parrot, two cats
And that will do.

You know I don't like spiders
With long, hairy legs.

Knowing my luck
I'd find it in your bed.

Spiders are creepy and crawly too,
But if you're good I will take you to see
Them at the zoo.'

Josh Davies (9)
Eccleston CE Primary School, Chester

I'm Like You!

I wish my teacher's eyes wouldn't roll past me
It's okay to praise me when I've done right,
I am just like you.

I should not be treated differently than all the rest
Because of my background
We are all different and God loves us all
Unlike some other people
I am just like you.

I wish I could be educated to the best
And earn good money and not sink to lick boots
I am just like you.

I wish I could walk on every criss-cross way of the globe
And no people or powers could get in my way because
I am just like you!

Josh Horrocks (10)
Eccleston CE Primary School, Chester

My Day At Wimbledon

The furry tennis ball is whacked side to side
Suddenly the match is won
The crowd stand and cheer
Oh no, here comes the rain again!
The groundsmen do their job
Court one's net goes down, the covers on
The players take a break
But centre court roof goes across
And the match plays on.

James Bowler (7)
Eccleston CE Primary School, Chester

Love

Love is a great thing
It makes me want to sing
I feel as though my heart is on fire
I think it is a desire
I feel as though it's a sweet
It is a great big treat
Love is a great thing
I feel as though I'm near to being king
I'm jumping with desire
And that to me is love.

Rebekah Kelly (9)
Eccleston CE Primary School, Chester

Tigers

T errifying tigers chase their prey
I ncisors as big as pins
G iant legs to run really fast
E ars to listen for human footsteps
R unning as fast as if trying to race a cheetah
S eeing their cubs, they run to protect them.

Holly Shaw (9)
Eccleston CE Primary School, Chester

Debbie The Duck

Debbie the duck, feathers yellow
Orange beak, paddle feet.
Swims on the pond
By the garden seat.
She is my pet, I love her so
We play together, she pecks my toe.

Skye Paul (10)
Eccleston CE Primary School, Chester

Seasons

Spring
Flowers blooming among the grass
Pansies, daisies, a wild mass.
Lambs playing, jumping high
Butterflies, bees and wasps pass by.

Summer
Sun burning hot and bright
Tanning treetops a beautiful sight
Children swimming in the pool
Having fun in here, it's very cool.

Autumn
Leaves falling different shades
Toffee crunch and marmalade
Wind howling through the trees
Whirling, drifting in the breeze.

Winter
Frost lying on the ground
Cold and misty, not a sound
Calendars opened every day
And if it snows you can go and play.

Anna Fearnall (10)
Eccleston CE Primary School, Chester

Wolves

The wolves are grey and live happily in the gloomy woods
In the daytime they play quietly in the snow
At night their upright ears listen for sounds
They hunt large animals and attack and kill them
The wolves howl deeply to each other
In the quiet, glistening, moonlit night.

Grace Rowland (9)
Eccleston CE Primary School, Chester

Sleeping

Lying on my perfect cushion,
Purring away while sleeping.
Suddenly I'm woken up
By a dog who's madly leaping.

So then I realise,
The freshness of the morning's here
The golden sun is leaking in
And my water is so clear.

I'm miaowing to my master
I'm starving really I am
So then the little girl wakes up
And asks me, 'Chicken or ham?'

Now I have my precious nap,
For an hour or two
Lying on my perfect cushion,
Next, it's more than a few.

Polly Mackarel (10)
Eccleston CE Primary School, Chester

Henry VIII

Henry VIII had six wives
One called Catherine, one called Jane,
If I had six wives it would be a pain.

Henry smells really bad
And he'll drive you mad,
Anne Boleyn was beheaded
Her execution day she dreaded.

Anne of Cleaves was divorced
She was not the first of course
Catherine Parr naturally died,
But she very nearly survived.

Alexander Thomas (8)
Eccleston CE Primary School, Chester

My Family

My sister is a nice little girl
She always likes her hair in curls.
My dad lies about his age
And his fave colour is beige.
My mum is kind and caring
Sometimes slightly daring.
My big sister has got a boyfriend
Their new house is on the mend.
My cousins are funny, they sleep with toy bunnies
My dad's family is so kind
They like me to use my mind.
My mum's family is so cool,
They have a big swimming pool!
I love my family.

Jenny Tilston (8)
Eccleston CE Primary School, Chester

Wolf

Forest lurcher
Clever smirker
Deer stalker
Wood walker
Teeth snapper
Bone cruncher
Moon howler
Enemy growler
Big ear
Keen hearer
Midnight walker
Daylight snorer.

Rhys Williams (10)
Eccleston CE Primary School, Chester

Egypt

Tutankhamen's mask of gold
Pyramids are very old
Tutankhamen was a king
Cats were worshipped above everything.

Everybody has a cat
That lays down on their mat
The cats drink lots of milk
Then lie down on their beds of silk.

The robbers steal a dead king's treasures
Pyramids need better safety measures
Had the robbers not done these things
We wouldn't know the wonders of the Egyptian kings.

Henry Makings (8)
Eccleston CE Primary School, Chester

The Hawk

The hawk swoops down to catch its prey
And then goes back east.
East is a lovely place
It grows flowers
Hawks live there
Soon the hawk flew to Australia
He went all around the universe
Some hawks are white
Some hawks are brown
Everywhere they go
They're bound to be the clown.

Matthew Booth (8)
Eccleston CE Primary School, Chester

My Family

My dad is so rude,
He stands up and watches the news.
My dad lies about his age
And his favourite colour is beige.
My mum is so cool,
She lets me do anything
And doesn't try to rule me.
My mum is kind,
She lets my friends come over.
My nanny is so nice, she lets me know
When it's time to paint and sew.
She lets me sleep over
My grandad lets me pick his potatoes
And tomatoes, when they have gone over.
I am allowed to walk Cassey his dog
Through the woods and over the logs.
My three dogs, all day they sleep
When I go to school and leave them I weep.
Murphy, Buster and Louis are small
But I manage to play with them all
And I love them all.

Portia Kitney (8)
Eccleston CE Primary School, Chester

Horses

Racing across the field, his chestnut fur sticky
Underneath the heavy saddle.
His clumpy hooves full with mud
Which after the pick will attack.
His tatty mane flying like a bird
Faster and faster, jumping any object.

Megan Gittings (9)
Eccleston CE Primary School, Chester

Ancient Egypt

Tutankhamen's mask stuffed with myrrh,
treasures and gold
pyramids are very old.

Mummifying bodies, disgusting stuff
if I did it I would be chuffed.

The Egyptians used to worship cats
but those cats didn't scratch.

Egypt is boiling hot,
even hotter than fire in a pot.

James Baker (9)
Eccleston CE Primary School, Chester

Christmas

C is for crackers going pop and bang
H is for happy when people open their presents
R is for reindeer guiding Santa's sleigh
I is for ivy growing all around us
S is for Santa who gives us all our presents
T is for turkey who gets the wish
M is for mistletoe who has to kiss
A is for advent calendar who gets the chocolate
S is for snow, soft and gentle.

Samuel Squires (7)
Eccleston CE Primary School, Chester

Love

Love is a great thing
I can kiss my mum and dad
I think love is wonderful
God loves us all
Love makes me happy
I love love, it's fantastic!

Andrew Bolton (7)
Eccleston CE Primary School, Chester

Our Head Teacher

Our head teacher always smiles
On her desk she has lots of files.

She eats her peach,
Then gets ready to teach.

Today is the day,
So hip hip hooray.

She wears lovely clothes
And loves to pose.

That's our head teacher!

Lucy Fearnall (8)
Eccleston CE Primary School, Chester

Egypt

Tutankhamen was the king
He asked his servant to stand up and sing.
The river Nile was a gift
But it could give you a very good lift.
Every Egyptian had a home
But it didn't have a phone.
Pyramids are very tall
I bet the king has a fancy, big hall.
Egyptians make papyrus boats
They might have worn furry coats.

Luke Faulkner (8)
Eccleston CE Primary School, Chester

Lara

Lara's fur is as black as night
Her eyes are shining, green and bright
She always has her prey in sight
Those poor mice she gives them such a fright.

Lauren Ellis (7)
Eccleston CE Primary School, Chester

Apples

The red, shiny apple
Rises up high
Ready to fall
From the big blue sky.

Then the wind
Comes round
And the apple
Hits the ground.

Hari Griffith (7)
Eccleston CE Primary School, Chester

Egypt

Tutankhamen's mask of gold
Found in his tomb
Very famous
Pyramids tall and old
Still surviving through the storms
Tombs buried
Treasures getting robbed.

James Austin (9)
Eccleston CE Primary School, Chester

My Pony

Misty is her name
Being grumpy is her game
She tries to bite
With all her might
But I love her all the same.

Rowan Stuart (7)
Eccleston CE Primary School, Chester

Playtime

Playtime is where kids have a break from their class
The boys play football on the grass
The girls play on the swings
Until the bell goes *ding!*

Sometimes the children eat their break outside
They run around and hide
The teachers stand and watch us play
And when it is time to go in they say, 'Hip hip hooray!'

Katy Evans (8)
Eccleston CE Primary School, Chester

Best Friends

Alice, Lucy and Lily are three best friends
If Alice and Lily fall out, Lucy will put them back together again.
Lucy, Alice and Lily are three best friends
No one can break them up, they sometimes disagree but not for long.
Lily, Lucy and Alice are three best friends
Everyone knows that they stand up for each other if ever they get into
trouble
Alice, Lucy and Lily are three best friends as everybody knows!

Lily Bissell (8)
Eccleston CE Primary School, Chester

Racing Cars

On the starting grid you wait for the lights to turn green
Go out, deafened by the roar of the engine behind your seat.
You grip the wheel tightly, breathe deeply, concentrate,
Hit the accelerator, the battle for the podium has begun!

Nelson Hughes (9)
Eccleston CE Primary School, Chester

Football

They pass the ball to each other
They run up the field towards the goal
Shoot and score
The other team went up the pitch
The shot went wide
The goalkeeper kicked the ball up the pitch
And went out for a throw-in.

Luke Rowland (7)
Eccleston CE Primary School, Chester

Football

Football is my favourite game
I wish Rooney was my name.
Then with just a little flick
I could score my first hat-trick.
Then I shall be very glad
Now I am off to tell my dad.

Thomas Rose (8)
Eccleston CE Primary School, Chester

Sleepy Grandpa

Sleepy Grandpa, you can hear him snore
Out the window and under the door.
TV's loud but he can't hear
Because he's snoring in his beer.
Come on Grandpa, time to wake
Mummy's making your favourite cake.

Edward Adams (7)
Eccleston CE Primary School, Chester

Where Skeletons Lie

Where skeletons lie
Souls have died
When tombs are laid
The vicar gets paid
When the bells do ring
The choir do sing
When you die
People cry.
Imprisoned in a coffin
Forever, amen.

Calum West (10)
Eccleston CE Primary School, Chester

The Rustling Wind

On an autumn day I dream of being on the clouds
When I walk through the rustling leaves the air rushes on my face
The autumn leaves shine in the sunshine
The autumn leaves crushed in your hand
The rustling wind snatches the leaves right out of my hand.

Jamie Handley (9)
Eccleston CE Primary School, Chester

Tea

Mummy said, 'I would love a cup of tea.'
She said, 'Tim, would you make one for me?'
I said, 'Now let me see
Yes of course, I'll make a cup of tea for thee.'

Timothy Tipping (8)
Eccleston CE Primary School, Chester

My Brother - Ismail

Ismail is my brother,
We play on the computer.
This makes me feel glad,
Until my dad says,
'Your eyes will be like squares.'

Ismail makes me laugh,
In the funniest way.
This makes me feel glad
Until my dad says,
'You laugh just like hyenas.'

Ismail gives me sweets,
They are such a treat.
This makes me feel glad,
Until my dad says,
'Your teeth will be like rotten sweetcorn.'

Ismail watches 'The Simpsons'
He acts just like Bart.
This makes me feel glad
Until my dad says,
'Your brain will be like mashed potato.'

Isaaq Mohammed (11)
Marsden CP School, Nelson

That's My Auntie

My auntie draws like an artist,
She is as colourful as a rainbow.
Her drawings are as beautiful as a waterfall
She is a real artist, that's my auntie!

She looks like she has just stepped out of a beauty parlour,
When she puts make-up on herself
She looks fine
She is an artist and a beauty
She is as beautiful as a Hollywood star
That's my auntie!

My auntie is the best cook in the world!
When I eat her cooked food I can't stop eating it.
It tastes better than chocolate or anything in the universe
She tells me I can eat it anytime I want,
That's my auntie!

The best thing about my auntie is that she never upsets me
And never shouts
She is the best
She is as kind as can be
That's my auntie!

Ummeya Zaka (9)
Marsden CP School, Nelson

My Dad

My dad always cheers me up, he's as happy as a clown.
When my dad laughs, it makes me want to laugh.
My dad is the best dad in the world.
He is so big, he could easily win the world's strongest man.
My dad is so important to me.

When my dad shouts, he looks like a buffalo
When my dad shouts, he makes me whimper,
I feel all tender and mild inside,
When my dad shouts, I feel furious and hurt,
I feel like kicking my dad.

I love it when my dad plays with me.
I feel as happy as a hippo when my dad is near.
I feel as important as the president.
I love it when my dad laughs, I feel like a princess.

I hate my dad when he shouts at me.
My dad is as mad as a madman when he shouts.
I feel like kicking my dad when he shouts.
I feel furious when my dad shouts.
I hate my dad when he shouts at me.

Bethany Owen (9)
Marsden CP School, Nelson

My Gran

Her face is as wrinkly as a scrunched up paper bag.
Her hair as comforting as my favourite quilt.
Gran's skin is as powdery as dry chapatti mix.
Her legs are as knobbly as twigs from a tree.
Her cuddles are as silver as a fifty pence piece.
Her eyes sparkle like sapphires.

Misbah J Ali (9)
Marsden CP School, Nelson

Mum

Mum always wakes me up and says, 'Rise and shine.'
I feel very, very happy,
Mum opens the curtains,
She is as pretty as a flower.

I always say, 'Goodbye,' and Mum always says it back,
I feel joyful,
Mum talks as sweet as an angel.

Mum always says, 'Goodnight,' and puts me to sleep
In bed and I feel warm,
Mum is as comfy as a teddy bear.

My mum always talks to me when I'm bored,
Mum cheers me up, I feel bright,
Her hair is as straight as a piece of leather.

Zeshan Mahmood (9)
Marsden CP School, Nelson

My Baby Sister

My sister is a great person to play with,
When she plays with me, she laughs like a clown,
She never stops because she is very playful.

When she's on the swings, she swings as high as a plane,
She never, ever fights with me,
She has a very infectious smile.

I feel sad when she cries,
She cries as loud as a blue whale,
When she cries I give her an immense hug.

When she stops crying, I cheer her up,
I cheer her up by telling her jokes like a comedian,
She just loves funny jokes.

Aqil Javed (8)
Marsden CP School, Nelson

My Brother

In the morning my brother wakes me up
He's jolly and excited
He's as fresh as a fish.

He eats as quick as a racing car so he can play with me
He doesn't want to play with my other brother
He's an Xbox bug.

I play with my cousin and my brother starts to cry
He cries like a waterfall
It makes me cry.

I play with my brother, he brightens up my day,
He's as funny as a clown, he's always happy
I love my little brother.

Sayra Gillani (9)
Marsden CP School, Nelson

My Holiday

I went on holiday
I flew up high
I never knew my mum would cry
It was a thirty minute journey.

When I got there I was scared
I never went on the beach and stared
I never went to the deep blue sea
Because there were jellyfish that came to me.

When I got to the place, I slept
I unpacked my stuff, then I wept
I put my clothes in the drawer,
I put my clothes in the closet.

I went to the pool
I sat on the stool
I went to my room
And stayed there till noon.

Jade Sherman (10)
Marsh Green Primary School, Wigan

In The Picture

Today I am going to school
And am going to be sitting on a stool
School is cool
And I am going to Liverpool
Next year I am going to high school
On a Sunday I go to school
Even though I want to go in the pool
My little sister goes to the nursery school
And she thinks it's cool!

My little brother watches cartoons
My dog popped my balloon
In June
Every night I see the full moon.
I am seeing my dad soon
I am seeing my dad in the middle of June.

Natalie Hewitt (11)
Marsh Green Primary School, Wigan

In The Picture

M is for motorbikes, fast machines
O ut on the open fields
T is for tyres gripping on the road
O for objects that you ride around
R is for rally bikes
B is for brakes to make me stop
I the ignition to start the bike
K is for the kit you wear
E is for engine, I hope my bike works!

David Glynn
Marsh Green Primary School, Wigan

Playgrounds

I'd like to be a friendship in the playground
Kindness whizzing round.
I'd like to whizz round a rally track
Which would come without a sound.
I'd like to see no bullies
Everyone being friends.
I'd like a farm
With lots of hens.
I'd like a fair
Which lasted all year long.
I'd like us to be happy
And sing a happy song.
I'd like to see no uniform
All year long.
I'd like a bell
Which went ding-dong.

Danielle Searle (9)
Mossley CE (VC) Primary School, Congleton

The Haunted Mansion

The building is so big and tall,
You feel as though you're going to fall.

You walk right in through the door,
You go right through the creaky floor.

You're not scared, you may boast,
But have you seen our creepy ghosts?

Walk a little further and you may see,
That you are scared and so are we.

So if you're not careful and not very wise,
You'll end up like a plate of fries.

Louise Walley (10)
Mossley CE (VC) Primary School, Congleton

Twelve Ways Of Looking At A Ladybird

Ladybirds, they are sweeter than a puppy,
Sweeter than the bright red poppy
I am growing in my room.
They have a funny face,
And a body spottier than my freckles,
They have a bright wide smile.
They dance a strange dance,
As they munch on leaves with their soft teeth.
They are as small as a mini stone
And as beautiful as a butterfly,
With the most bright and beautiful wings.
Antennae as long as an eyelash,
Spotty black spots fluttering in the air.
If I was an aphid I would scatter away as fast as I could,
I would scatter away until my legs fell off.
Every day, they come walking up to us aphids,
And munching like an electric knife.
They are as little as a lead
And have rolling, beady eyes.
They have eyes as bright as the sun
And have legs like string,
But are as fast as an athlete.
They are as active as a Fiesta
And are as bright as fire.
If I was an aphid I would see one as a giant,
If I could turn myself into a bird I would eat them.
They are always munching on leaves
As happy as a butterfly.

Alice Jones (8)
Mossley CE (VC) Primary School, Congleton

Our Playground

I would like more goals
To play football
I would like more space to play games
To play catch
I would like more sharing
To make sure I get a go
I would like more toys
To make sure I get a toy
I would like more friends
To play with
I would like more food to share
To have a snack
I would like more benches
To have a sit down.

Aaron Nuttall (9)
Mossley CE (VC) Primary School, Congleton

Playground Poem

I would like to have a rally track.
If I had gold and silver
I would have a big house.
It would be better if we had more space.
It would be so much fun if people shared.
If people were kind no one would be sad.
Do you agree?
I said do you agree?
If you agree say yowl to me!

George Harper (8)
Mossley CE (VC) Primary School, Congleton

Six Ways To Look At An Aardvark

One
Aardvarks smell as good as a lion
And the smell never stops.

Two
Aardvarks are as lazy
As little cats.

Three
Ants must be terrified
When the aardvark's sticky tongue
Comes out to eat them.

Four
Aardvark's ears are as long as rabbits
And drop down to the grass.

Five
Aardvarks are as cute
And small as dogs.

Six
His legs are as strong
As big elephants.

Hollie Kiely (8)
Mossley CE (VC) Primary School, Congleton

My Playground Poem

I'd like a great roller coaster
that went whizzing all around.
I'd like a very muddy rally track on the ground.
I'd like a bigger playground.
I'd like to come to school in my own clothes.
I wish there was a Burger King
and everything was for free.

Ellis Frodsham (9)
Mossley CE (VC) Primary School, Congleton

Five Ways Of Looking At A Shark

One
A shark can smell
As far as a hare.

Two
Flashing red eyes
Just like a flame.

Three
Killer teeth red and white
Like a diamond in the sky.

Four
Big belly
Like a cloud in the sky.

Five
A shark, powerful
As a whip.

Adam Ball (8)
Mossley CE (VC) Primary School, Congleton

My Playground Poem

I'd like a track that went whizz, whizz
I'd like some Coke that went fizz, fizz
I'd like giant candyfloss because I'm the boss
I'd like lots of Haribo yum-yum in my tum
I'd like bubblegum grass, I like it sweet and sour
I'd like a chocolate bunny hopping in my tummy
I'd like to run around my playground.

John Evans (8)
Mossley CE (VC) Primary School, Congleton

Seven Ways To Look . . .

One
Swift as lightning,
Faster than the eye can see
No man has ever seen.

Two
A tail plated with steel,
Balancing the body
Never fallen.

Three
Ears sharp
Hearing everything
In the country.

Four
No manners at all
Teeth as sharp as razors
Always on the kill.

Five
Spots black as a black hole
Round as an eye
Black as a rain cloud.

Six
Fur as soft as a little lamb
Fire fur but soft as a lamb.

Seven
The ultimate runner
Of time
Which nothing has seen.

(A cheetah.)

Jordan Grocott (8)
Mossley CE (VC) Primary School, Congleton

Eight Ways To Look At A Cheetah

One
It eats like a pig
With absolutely no manners at all.

Two
His skin has black spots on it
As black as a black hole

Three
His legs are as fast as a jet engine
Maybe even faster.

Four
His ears always pricked up for trouble.
They are also as sharp as elves' ears.

Five
Its tail used for balance
Is also as hard as steel.

Six
Its belly is more fluffy
Than a lamb.

Seven
His teeth as yellow
As a bottle of yellow food colouring.

Eight
As spotty as a gorilla's
Trouble-making face.

James Ball (9)
Mossley CE (VC) Primary School, Congleton

My Cute Dolphin

They catch food with their tongue
Like pelicans when they fly.

They have a water spout
Coming out of their tummy
Like my sister spitting.

They squeak when they're scared
Like my cat when I stand on his tail.

They are cute like puppies
Because they kiss underwater.

They do acrobatics
Like clowns at a circus.

They sleep so stiffly
Like a shipwreck under water.

They splash like speedboats
Splashing away.

They have big eyes like diamonds
Sparkling in the sea.

They breathe like my dad snoring
Just like when he sleeps for three days.

They've a rough tummy
Like sandpaper that hurts.

They swim fast like a motorbike
Zooming.

They have tiny baby teeth
Even though they're old, like my mum.

They are harmless,
They cannot hurt you, like chicks.

They catch their prey
From the ocean like lions.

Emma Roxburgh (7)
Mossley CE (VC) Primary School, Congleton

Eight Ways To Look At A Rattlesnake

One
Produces poison,
Like a dirty river flowing fast.

Two
It cannot hear its own rattle
It is deaf.

Three
It sneaks under the long grass
To catch its prey.

Four
Its skin is as soft
As a six inch ball of silk.

Five
It is as shiny as a crystal diamond
Shining in the moonlight.

Six
It eats very small creatures
Like rats and kangaroos.

Seven
It is a reptile that chews you up
Into diddy pieces and spits you out.

Eight
It feels horrid to be poisoned by a rattlesnake
It strikes its poison into me and I die.

Kyle McLellan (8)
Mossley CE (VC) Primary School, Congleton

Ten Ways of Looking At An Aardvark

One
Aardvarks' ears are as big as rabbits',
Dangling down on the ground.

Two
Aardvarks are as cute
As dogs.

Three
Digging up nests and eating termites,
Mud everywhere.

Four
Baby aardvarks drink milk
As white as snow.

Five
Aardvarks' holes as good as moles
Really, really deep.

Six
Aardvarks' fur as soft as sheep
Like a woolly cardigan.

Seven
Aardvarks are as lazy as cats
Sitting on the bed.

Eight
Aardvarks' eyes twinkle like stars
Way up high.

Nine
Aardvarks' smell is as good as lions'
That is a really good sense of smell.

Ten
Aardvarks' claws are as sharp
As crocodiles' teeth scratching trees.

Danielle Tatton (8)
Mossley CE (VC) Primary School, Congleton

Ladybird Madness

Ladybirds are as spotty as a person with three freckles
On each side of their face.

She dances a strange dance,
Like a person does on a dance mat, only scuttery.

The ladybird's legs are as scuttery as a beetle,
Out of balance on a cranky, cranky bush.

The ladybird has a bright body,
When she flies her body is like a big light bulb lit up.

The ladybird has got a big smile like a smiley sticker.

Ladybird has got legs like little chunks of string chopped up in bits.

The ladybird's back is as red as a rose.

When the ladybird flies its wings are beautiful
Because it looks like a colour wheel.

The ladybird is as small as a lump of lead out of a pencil.

The ladybird is as fast as athletic, little, sweet bugs.

Ladybirds are as active as a little, small Fiesta on a rally.

Ladybirds look like sunshine in the air because they are bright.

Ladybird are as sweet as poppies
Because they don't bite you and they are red.

A ladybird is as small as a baby stone in some mud.

Rebecca Jackson (8)
Mossley CE (VC) Primary School, Congleton

Nine Ways To Look At A Spider

One
Biting, sneaking up to the dinner,
then snap, it has gone,
just like a snake.

Two
Pincers squeaky clean,
when it's coming to you,
they pinch you like a needle.

Three
His eyes shine,
in the dark,
they're black as night.

Four
They are hairy,
very hairy,
just like a gorilla.

Five
They run,
a long distance,
they run like a cheetah.

Six
Stuck in a web,
that would be a shock,
slimy, shiny, silky and invisible.

Seven
They eat insects and other things that I'm talking about,
they are awful,
they eat with their pincers.

Eight
They come in bright colours
at least some do,
there are two kinds.

Nine
The other kind are poisonous,
they are very delicate,
and I hate them.

What I have been talking about is a spider,
and tarantula,
there are nine ways to look at a spider.

Megan Hogg (8)
Mossley CE (VC) Primary School, Congleton

Eight Ways Of Looking At A Spider

The pincers are as poisonous as a pit viper
When it is angry because someone has got away.

Its patterns are as red as blood
In a crash with red-hot fire.

Its eight legs are as freaky as frogs' legs.
Its eight legs are as quick as Steven Gerrard.

Its hair is as prickly as a thorn bush
And its hair is as black as the night sky.

The legs are as long as sticks
And as thin as hair.

In a spider's tummy you feel sick and gruesome
Like a great white shark.

The web is as messy as a pencil pot
And sticky like a sticker.

The redback is as bloodthirsty as a robber
And as nasty as the minotaur.

Luke Harpur (8)
Mossley CE (VC) Primary School, Congleton

Eleven Ways Of Looking At A Spider

One
Spiders move quickly like the wind
They move as fast as my car.

Two
Spiders have really good eyesight
Like my cat's eyes.

Three
Spiders are very hairy
Just like my dad's beard
That he hasn't shaved for a long time.

Four
Spiders spin a web to catch flies
Like you have been tangled up
In some string.

Five
Spiders wrap their legs around dinner
Like someone is wrapping you
Around into a ball.

Six
Spiders, they seek blood out of the flies
And they just lay there
All crispy in the web.

Seven
Sticky webs covered in dew
Just like long, wavy grass.

Eight
Eight poisonous fangs to kill prey
Like a gun that's gone bang.

Nine
A little fly as still as a desk
Dreading its fears as it was dead.

Ten
Spiders are stronger than smaller animals
And they are terrified.

Eleven
Spiders are creepy
Like the night of Hallowe'en.

Lauren Myatt (8)
Mossley CE (VC) Primary School, Congleton

Eight Ways To Look At A Rattlesnake

One
It produces poison
Like a fast tap on full blast.

Two
It sneaks under grass
Like a little mouse to kill like fire.

Three
His skin is as smooth
As a ball of silk which my nanna knits with.

Four
It is as shiny as a diamond
Which my mum has on her earring.

Five
It eats small mammals,
It eats them like a dog chewing his bone.

Six
It is a reptile or a mammal
Like a dinosaur killing you and me.

Seven
Good day mate
I don't like being bitten by a rattlesnake.

Eight
It cannot hear its own rattle
Because it is deaf like a toy.

Andrew Kruze (8)
Mossley CE (VC) Primary School, Congleton

Eleven Ways Of Looking At A Spider

One
Spiders have good eyesight at night
For hunting like my cat.

Two
They suck blood
Like a hungry mosquito.

Three
Poisonous fangs
To kill its prey with.

Four
Spiders move quickly
Like the wind.

Five
Long legs to wrap up flies
To be stored away for winter.

Six
Spiders are creepy like Hallowe'en,
They spin a web that scares me.

Seven
Spiders are stronger
Than smaller animals.

Eight
Some spiders are very hairy.

Nine
Sticky web covered in dew.

Ten
A little fly still as a desk,
Dreading its fears but then he was dead.

Eleven
Sticky cobweb catching flies
The spider eats one as soon as it dies.

Hannah Johnson (7)
Mossley CE (VC) Primary School, Congleton

Six Ways Of Looking At A Spider

Spiders run like a cat running for freedom
In a big living room.

Spiders' webs are very big and sticky
Reaching up into the attic and all in my bedroom.

Spiders run as fast as a very big leopard
Running very fast.

Spiders' legs are as hairy
As a big gorilla.

Spiders bite,
Gruesome like sharks' teeth.

Spiders' eyes
Are as wobbly as eyes.

Thomas Derbyshire (9)
Mossley CE (VC) Primary School, Congleton

Playgrounds

I would like to have a bigger playground.
I would like slides in the playground.
I would like a fish pond in the playground.
I would like swings in the playground.
I would like a lot more friends in the playground.
I would like a swimming pool in the playground.

Charlotte Oakley (8)
Mossley CE (VC) Primary School, Congleton

Six Ways To Look At A Shark

As big as an elephant's leg or body
He has big legs.

The teeth are strong as a diamond
Diamonds are very strong.

Sharks are scary like a horrible goblin.

The tail is as strong as the Earth.

The teeth are as strong as a T-rex's.

It is as strong as a man picking up steel.

Kimberley Wilson (7)
Mossley CE (VC) Primary School, Congleton

Four Ways Of Looking At A Spider

Spiders, they move like my dad running
Just like if he plays badminton five times a day.

Spiders, they eat like my mum sleeping
Just like if she hasn't eaten for ten days.

Spiders, they crawl like my brother eating
Just like if he hasn't slept for two days.

Spiders, they fight like my sister kicking
Just like if she hasn't swam for seven days.

Isaac Pemberton (9)
Mossley CE (VC) Primary School, Congleton

Ten Ways Looking At A Spider

The redback spider is as bloodthirsty as the minotaur or a dinosaur.
The pincers are as poisonous as a dragon or a viper snake.
The redback hairs are as prickly as a thorn bush or a needle.
The hairs are as black as the night sky or dried lava.
The redback's spider's legs are as long as a stick
                                             and a tree put together.
The web is as sticky as a sticker or a jellyfish.
In a spider's tummy you feel sick and gruesome
                                             and you feel like a zombie.
Its patterns are as red as blood or a volcano eruption.
Its eight legs are as freaky as frogs' legs or a devil.
Its legs are as quick as Steven Gerrard or Zidane.

Daniel Loach (9)
Mossley CE (VC) Primary School, Congleton

Celebrate A Friend

I want to be friends with you
Till the sea drains away and till we die.

If we are friends, I will always be a good friend
And share my toys with you.

I will give you a teddy that I will buy you
And I will let you feed my fish when I come home.

I will like you more than Jenn,y my imaginary friend
And more than beautiful flowers.

Leah Carney (8)
Murdishaw West Community Primary School, Runcorn

What Is Pink?
(Based on 'What Is Pink' by Christina Rossetti)

What is pink? A petal is pink
floating in the brink.

What is red? A jelly is red
wobbling in my belly.

What is blue? The sea is blue
with the reflection of the sky.

What is white? Snow is white
making my fingers cold.

What is yellow? Honeydew melon is yellow
tasting better than ever.

What is green? Grass is green
for playing football.

What is violet? Flowers are violet
that sprout in the soil.

What is orange? Why an orange
just an orange.

Jordan Stoba (9)
Murdishaw West Community Primary School, Runcorn

Autumn

I see leaves falling off the tree.
I hear bees buzzing in the bush.
I taste cappuccino when I come in from school.
I smell smoke in the woods.
I feel crunching leaves in my hand.

Luke Reddington (8)
Murdishaw West Community Primary School, Runcorn

What Is Pink?
(Based on 'What Is Pink?' by Christina Rossetti)

What is pink? My skin is pink
It covers me from head to toe.

What is red? A rose is red
Smelling beautiful as well.

What is blue? Blueberries are blue
Are they tasty in a stew?

What is white? A dove is white
White, flying through the night.

What is green? The grass is green
The sweetest sight I've ever seen.

What is orange? Why an orange?
Just an orange.

Regan Jolliffe (8)
Murdishaw West Community Primary School, Runcorn

Celebrate A Friend

I want to be friends with you till I die
And I am in Heaven till the sea turns black.

If we are friends I will let you stand in front of me in the dinner line
I will let you pick a game to play at playtime.

I will give you a special toy
I will give you my mobile phone so you can ring me up.

I will like you more than my favourite chocolate
I will like you more than the flowers that are in my garden.

Samantha Kneale (9)
Murdishaw West Community Primary School, Runcorn

What Is Pink?
(Based on 'What Is Pink?' by Christina Rossetti)

What is pink? A flamingo is pink
Dipping its toes in the brink.

What is red? Strawberries are red
Growing in the garden bed.

What is blue? Bluebells are blue
Jingling all the time.

What is yellow? The sun is yellow
Shining through the clouds.

What is green? Trees are green
Swaying in the wind.

What is violet? Paper is violet
Getting used for art.

James Ward (8)
Murdishaw West Community Primary School, Runcorn

Celebrate A Friend

I want to be friends with you till we die.
If we are friends I will kill to be next to you,
I will give you what you need,
I will like you more than money,
More than life of the world that I am on all day
And the air that I use to keep me alive.

Lewis Hughes (9)
Murdishaw West Community Primary School, Runcorn

Autumn Sense Poem

I see lovely birch trees
Breaking in the wind.

I hear the squelchy noise
Of the mud splashing.

I taste creamy toffee apples
As I eat them.

I smell lovely, misty air
While I am walking.

I feel crinkly leaves underfoot
As I walk.

Gemma Lenahan (8)
Murdishaw West Community Primary School, Runcorn

Celebrate A Friend

I want to be friends with you
Till the sun sets in the morning.

If we are friends I will love you
Better than the scent of flowers
And the sound of the birds singing
In the summer trees.

I will be friends with you
Until we grow into old ladies
And until the busy ladybird
Loses its spots.

Alisha Parker (9)
Murdishaw West Community Primary School, Runcorn

My Sister

She is . . .
Sweet like the springtime flowers,
As much fun as a playtime that lasts many hours.

As sharp as a wolf's claw,
As orange as boiling hot shores.

Red, like the tasty cherry,
Saturdays because she's always merry.

Just like a saxophone or a loud speaking voice,
She likes drinks, have a choice!

She's a bookcase to tell me tales,
To be sunny as the darkness fails.

That's my sister Louise's tales!

Rachel Tompkins (8)
Overleigh St Mary's Primary School, Chester

My Cousin

You're bouncy and fuzzy like a pillow
You sway in the breeze like a willow.

Your season is summer because you're always bright
Your colour is yellow because you're ever so light.

Monday is your day because you're awakening and loud
Coke is your drink because you're lively and proud.

A monkey is your animal because you're bouncy and bright
You fly in the air like a soaring kite.

You are an alarm clock waking me up
You're comforting like a drink I sip out of my cup.

Amy Bebbington (8)
Overleigh St Mary's Primary School, Chester

My Teacher

She is happy and fun, like spring,
She shines like the stars at night.

She is the sun in summer,
She is calm but energetic like Saturday.

She is pink like a tulip,
She is a tiger who pounces on her prey.

She is the taste of Diet Coke that fizzes up
                                    with white froth.
She is the sound of laughter all day.

She is the soft cushion of a sofa
So . . .
Please don't take her away!

Freya Brewis (9)
Overleigh St Mary's Primary School, Chester

My Mum

You are the summer, happy and kind
You are a cat, calm, likes a nap.

You are Sunday, relaxed every day
You are like water, peaceful.

You are morning, sunny and ready
You are ripples of a calm lake, peaceful.

You are the colour yellow, sunny
You are like a bed, comfy and warm.

You are the sun, kind and shining
And nobody can replace you
'Cause you're my mum!

Seren Challand (8)
Overleigh St Mary's Primary School, Chester

My Cousin Brinsley

You're like summer
Always so happy.

You're like the sunset,
Because your suntan glows.

You're like the sun
Because you're so bright.

You're like the taste of strawberries,
Really sweet.

You're like the waves,
Because you're so outgoing.

You're like the butterfly,
Very pretty.

You're like the colour pink,
Such a girlie-girl.

You're like my sofa,
So comforting.

You're like a sports car,
Really jazzy.

You're like a Saturday,
Relaxed (sometimes)!

Anna Houghton (9)
Overleigh St Mary's Primary School, Chester

Haiku

Blue sea licks the shore,
Building a large sandcastle
It eats my building.

Amber Houlders (9)
Overleigh St Mary's Primary School, Chester

My Twin Brother

Mike is like a bike, he runs all round the room,
He's like a teddy, he comforts me at night,
And he's like Friday, very annoying,
He always hogs the cushion.

When I get him angry, he's like a ball of fire,
When I go to bed, he bangs his head on the bed
Like a bongo drum.

When we get a bottle of dandelion and burdock,
He's like a massive hoover,
He scoffs it all in one go!

David Cavendish (9)
Overleigh St Mary's Primary School, Chester

My Friend

He's as good as gold,
He is stony and bold.

He's as lively as a hare,
He's as bright as the sun.

He stays up as late as midnight,
He's as red as an apple, when he's angry.

He's as graceful as a willow,
But he's my friend.

James McDermott (8)
Overleigh St Mary's Primary School, Chester

The Shimmering Star

The shimmering star
Stays put in the sky,
Sparkly, glittery, pale.
No one knows how it got there,
It has stayed in its place for thousands of years.
It makes me feel small
When it hangs in the sky as big
as the other stars.
The shimmering star,
Reminds me that life is something
you'll keep.

Sophie Wilkin (10)
Overleigh St Mary's Primary School, Chester

And My Heart Soars

The dazzling of the moon,
The beauty of the flowers,
The gracefulness of the swans,
Speak to me.

The gentleness of the sea,
The laughter of the children,
The sweetness of the grass,
They speak to me and my heart soars.

Joseph Speed (8)
Overleigh St Mary's Primary School, Chester

The Luxurious Island

The luxurious island
It's thousands of islands put together
Magnificent, amazing, wonderful
Like magic
Like diamonds glowing through the sand
Makes me feel magical
Like happy dolphins in the sun
The luxurious island
Diving dolphins gliding through the shimmering water.

Merika Holmes (11)
Overleigh St Mary's Primary School, Chester

And My Heart Soars

The softness of the clouds,
The chattering of the children.
The dazzling of the stars
Speak to me.

The power of the voices,
The bareness of the body,
The sparkle of the eye
Speak to me.

Hannah Aird (8)
Overleigh St Mary's Primary School, Chester

Children

There are many different types of children
Some are timid and shy,
Some are nasty and sly.

Children have different personalities
Naughty, don't care, smirking,
Perfect, enthusiastic, working.

There are lots of different appearances
Tidy, neat and shiny hair,
And some that don't care what they wear.

There are good friendships and bad friendships,
Friendships that will always last,
Friendships remembered from the past.

But children are all the same,
It doesn't matter what you look like.
There is nothing wrong with untidy hair,
Or if you have a new bike.

Louise Tompkins (10)
Overleigh St Mary's Primary School, Chester

My Mum

You're like summer,
Happy, cheerful and refreshing.

You're like an evening candle,
Bright and welcoming.

You're like a dog,
Playful all the time.

You're like a soothing flute,
Very, very gentle.

You're like a glass of wine,
Always sweet and kind.

y Lawrence (8)
gh St Mary's Primary School, Chester

Luke

You are like Coca-Cola
Sweet and kind.
You are like my kitchen chair
Reliable when I'm down.
You are like Monday
Wild and almost uncontrollable.
You are like a fox
Gentle but wild.
You are like an alarm clock
Loud, but calming.
You are like the wind
Strong and powerful.
You are like autumn
Like the leaves, you are soft and gentle.
You are like red
The brightest of colours.
You are like lunchtime
Happy and sweet.

Peter O'Donoghue (8)
Overleigh St Mary's Primary School, Chester

Rachel

You are as bright and sunny as summer is,
You are as bouncy as a bouncing bean,
You are playtime, always going wild.
Excited as a tabby cat, jumping all around,
You are purple, a calming colour, right for your night,
You are Sunday fun, like Sunday school.
You are the sound of laughing and jumping, a jolly sound,
You are a peaceful armchair sitting there alone,
Your hair is gold like the autumn leaves, swaying in the breeze.

Jenny Thomas (9)
Overleigh St Mary's Primary School, Chester

Robert

He is like a cushion,
nice and comforting.
Like an alarm clock,
mad and loud.

Like the sun,
lovely and bright.
Like a Sunday,
peaceful and calm.

Like beautiful yellow,
hot and warm.
Like a spotty cheetah,
speedy and fast.

Like the afternoon
out and about.
Like the pepperoni on a pizza,
sizzling and boiling.

Like the summer,
funny and amusing.

Jennifer Williams (8)
Overleigh St Mary's Primary School, Chester

Me

I'm warm like the summer,
I smile like the shining sun.

I'm fizzy like Fanta,
My hair is the blondeness of a cheetah.

I'm smooth and bouncy like a sofa,
The blueness of my eyes is the sea.

The sound of laughter is around me all day,
I'm afternoon, near to the end of the school day.

I'm Fridays, tired and ready to go home.

Lucy Powell (9)
Overleigh St Mary's Primary School, Chester

My Sister Lottie

You're autumn
Running like mad

You're Coke
Bubbling around

You're a tiger
Bouncing about

Your colour is orange
Always happy and bright

You are a bed
Cuddly and soft

You are the wind
Wild all the time

You're an alarm clock
Waking me up.

Elizabeth Cousins (8)
Overleigh St Mary's Primary School, Chester

My Literacy Teacher

As bright as the morning
As sharp as a wolf's teeth

As clear as water
White like snow

Like a bookcase full of information
As loud as a saxophone

The start of the week
As colourful as autumn
As boring as a rainy day.

Esther Maiden (8)
Overleigh St Mary's Primary School, Chester

Anna

My sister Anna is as cheeky as a monkey,
and is brilliant at hide and seek.
She loves shoes that make a noise,
she calls them clippy-cloppy shoes!

She's like the spring, funny and warm,
like the spring blue sky is her smile
and the rain is like her tears.

She's like a pancake in a pan,
warm and fiery.
She's never tired, but always up early.
She reminds me of a colourful rainbow.

Lily Wearden (8)
Overleigh St Mary's Primary School, Chester

My Sister Elizabeth

Your season is definitely spring,
Alive, always alive.

You're as bubbly as lemonade
Bubbly, bubbly in your tummy.

You're so much fun
Fun like Fridays.

You're always bouncy
Bouncy as a bed.

You're as loud as a trumpet
But as cuddly as a panda bear.

Kathryn Cowley (8)
Overleigh St Mary's Primary School, Chester

The Enchanted Forest

The enchanted forest,
It's a magical place, where
Anything can happen.
Mysterious, powerful and special.
A fairy tale land where anything
Can come true.
A place where mythical creatures
Roam when dreams become reality.
It makes me feel curious,
I am a vision in my imagination
That lurks in the shadows of the forest.
The enchanted forest.
It reminds me of a fairy-tale land.

Jade Robson (11)
Overleigh St Mary's Primary School, Chester

And My Heart Soars

The softness of the sparkling sand,
The glistening of the white snow.
The swaying of the green trees
Speak to me.

The shining of the red sunset,
The weaving of the blue sea.
The darkness of the blue sky,
They speak to me.

Leah Newell
Overleigh St Mary's Primary School, Chester

The Highwayman
(Based on 'The Highwayman' by Alfred Noyes)

He was not seen at sunset
He was not seen at dawn,
Bess, the landlord's daughter, felt
As though her heart had been torn.
She clutched the musket trigger
In her quivering hand,
Then a horse and a man came galloping,
Galloping, galloping
Then a horse and a man came galloping
Up to the innkeeper's land.

Callum Boyd (9)
Overleigh St Mary's Primary School, Chester

And My Heart Soars

The breeze in the blue sky,
The joy of your family.
The brightness of the sun,
Speak to me.

The trees swaying about,
The softness of the deep sand.
The twinkling of the stars
Speak to me and my heart soars.

Sumera Sharif (7)
Overleigh St Mary's Primary School, Chester

The Highwayman
(Based on 'The Highwayman' by Alfred Noyes)

Peering through the window to see my lady standing bright,
Her fingers threading through her hair, gleaming with a light.
The tassels on my lady's dress sparkling in the midnight moon,
The twinkle of the midnight sky, flying by, flying by.
The twinkling of the midnight sky, preparing for her doom.

The highwayman comes knocking, knocking on the old inn door,
To see his lady princess standing in rich galore.
And what he sees is there to please -.
As the midnight moon is shining, shining,
As the midnight moon is shining over the swaying trees.

Anna L Grainger (10)
Overleigh St Mary's Primary School, Chester

And My Heart Soars

The grace of the butterfly,
The glimmer of the sea.
The waving of the trees
Speak to me.

The whisper of my friends,
The thunder of the sky.
The munching of my food
They speak to me
And my heart soars.

Isabella Brown (8)
Overleigh St Mary's Primary School, Chester

The Crumbling Castle

The crumbling castle
Built hundreds of years ago
Towering, dazzling, daring
Like an old monument, standing tall
Like a rock slide about to fall
It makes me feel young
Like a new baby has just been born
The crumbling castle
What man can do!

Abbey Badaei (11)
Overleigh St Mary's Primary School, Chester

And My Heart Soars!

The beauty of the friendship,
The force of the wave.
The freshness of the sun,
Speak to me.

The care of my friends,
The fun of swimming.
The beauty of a butterfly,
They speak to me and my heart soars.

Samuel Davies (8)
Overleigh St Mary's Primary School, Chester

And My Heart Soars

The kindness of my friends,
The brightness of the sun.
The love of my family
Speak to me.

The fun of comedy
Going somewhere else when you go on holiday.
The kindness of my grandma
They speak to me,
And my heart soars.

Alice Johnson (7)
Overleigh St Mary's Primary School, Chester

And My Heart Soars

The calmness of the river
The hope of family and friends,
The beauty of a flower
Speak to me.

The softness of the sand
The view of the mountain,
The quietness of the evening
They speak to me
And my heart soars.

Amelia Jones (8)
Overleigh St Mary's Primary School, Chester

The Leaning Tower Of Pisa

The tall tower of Pisa,
Leaning awkwardly over the land.
Tall, breathtaking, famous.
Like an unstable skyscraper.
Like a Jenga tower about to tumble.
Makes me feel small,
Small like an insect.
The Tower of Pisa
Shows us what wonderful things man can do.

Ben Preston (10)
Overleigh St Mary's Primary School, Chester

The Jazzy Saxophone

The jazzy saxophone
It has six smooth pearl buttons
Loud, stylish, shiny
Like the noise of an echoed castle
Like a curve of a rainbow
It makes me feel like a famous musician
It makes me want to get up and dance
The jazzy saxophone
How beautiful music can be.

Jasmine Blythin (10)
Overleigh St Mary's Primary School, Chester

The Golden Eagle

The golden eagle,
The biggest preying bird,
Striking, huge, rare.
Like a jet soaring through the sky.
Like a giant hawk hunting for its prey.
It makes me feel afraid.
Like a squirrel about to be swooped upon.
The golden eagle,
A mighty bird.

Adam Kassab (11)
Overleigh St Mary's Primary School, Chester

The Great Eiffel Tower

The great Eiffel Tower
Expands in the summer.
Huge, phenomenal, shocking.
Like an ancient pyramid.
Like a statue in the clouds.
Makes me feel minute,
Minute like an ant pushed aside and ignored.
The great Eiffel Tower,
Reminds us of our size.

Isaac Jones (10)
Overleigh St Mary's Primary School, Chester

The Galloping Horse

The galloping horse,
Galloping horses are all over our land.
Beautiful, amazing and intelligent.
They are like boomerangs, they can gallop
But always come back, one time or another.
Like my demon, always there beside and
watching over me.
I feel like I am their mum, well to me I am
all animals' mum.
They make me feel like I am on top of the world.
The galloping horses,
All that's on my mind, is animals.

Lily Walton (11)
Overleigh St Mary's Primary School, Chester

The Ancient Fort

The ancient fort
A thousand years older
Tall, old, wide,
Like a huge statue.
Like a monument, standing tall.
How short life is
Like a small ant standing next to it
The ancient fort
The guards stopped it from becoming ruins.

Douglas Kent (10)
Overleigh St Mary's Primary School, Chester

The Sun

The sun
The brightest star in the sky
Hot, fiery, scorching.
It's like the bulb of the Earth
It's like the lamp of the gods.
Warm, ecstatic and lively.
It makes my garden a tropical paradise.
The sun
Life-giver of the world.

Hannah Lord (11)
Overleigh St Mary's Primary School, Chester

My Little Brother

My littler brother
He was born in 1999.
Small, intelligent, loveable.
Like a brave boy.
Like an angel.
He makes me feel happy.
He makes me feel huge and towering.
My little brother,
He reminds us how strongly loved we are.

Amy Landsborough (10)
Overleigh St Mary's Primary School, Chester

And My Heart Soars

The colours of flowers,
The softness of the clouds
The sweetness of the tulips
Speak to me.

The lightness of the rain,
The blazing of the sun,
The turquoise of the sea
Speak to me.

The laughter of the children,
The greenness of the trees,
The whiteness of the swans
Speak to me.

Alex Halliwell-Dykes (8)
Overleigh St Mary's Primary School, Chester

Guinea Pig

Guinea pig
Resting in his home
Cute, cuddly, stubborn
Like a lawnmower
Mowing up the lawn
Like an innocent civilian
Sitting in a hutch
It makes me feel sorry
Like a homeless dog
On the street
A hero to the guinea pig.

Matthew Harle (11)
Overleigh St Mary's Primary School, Chester

My Cat Charlie

Charlie is all colours,
He's very careful where he goes.
Charlie is very long when he stretches
He makes no sound whatsoever.
Charlie has sharp claws
But soft paws
Charlie creeps up to a bird
He waits,
He jumps . . . and Charlie gets a bullseye!
Charlie bounces just like a spring,
That's Charlie!

Daisy A Speed (9)
Overleigh St Mary's Primary School, Chester

Tiger, Tiger

Tiger, tiger
With different coloured stripes
Lives under the traffic lights.
No tiger has ever been
Coloured red and green.
He's shy but fierce
He never has tears.
But the only thing that is wrong -
And this may sound like a song,
But when the amber is the light,
Everyone can see him bright.

Flora McWilliam (9)
Overleigh St Mary's Primary School, Chester

The Falling Snow

The falling snow
Made out of ice
Delicate, soft, beautiful
Like Heaven coming down to Earth
Like a peaceful dream
I feel chilly and icy
Like a frozen icicle
The falling snow
It makes you feel like
You're in Heaven.

Sophie Powell (11)
Overleigh St Mary's Primary School, Chester

And My Heart Soars

The scaliness of the crocodiles,
The softness of the clouds.
The hopping of the toads
Speak to me.

The roar of the lion,
The scent of the flowers,
The grace of the swans
And the smoothness of the mud
Speak to me.

Rhiannon Owen (7)
Overleigh St Mary's Primary School, Chester

The Valley - Haiku

Mountains watching down,
Lake filled with beauty and peace,
Like a lovely child.

Alec Shuttleworth (10)
Overleigh St Mary's Primary School, Chester

The Lady Of Shalott
(Based on 'The Lady Of Shalott' by Alfred Lord Tennyson)

Down a river in the boat she flows,
She knows not where the river goes.
In the moonlight she always shows
Under her gown, her shivering toes.
Away from tower'd Camelot,
She tries to shout, nothing comes out.
She tries to listen but hears nowt.
Now she dies, full of doubt.
The Lady o' Shalott.

Danny Ward (10)
Overleigh St Mary's Primary School, Chester

And My Heart Soars

The singing of the birds,
The glory of the flowers,
The saltiness of the sea
Speak to me.

The sparkling of the stars
The hotness of the sun,
The freshness of the air
Speak to me.

Adam Thomson (8)
Overleigh St Mary's Primary School, Chester

Tsunami

Here in Great Britain, people raising money
Down in far-off countries, life is all but sunny
Turmoil, pain and sadness
Lives turned upside-down
Homes and buildings crushed
Everything once green, has turned to horrid brown

It makes me feel so lucky to have all my lovely things
A new bike, a warm house and all that Santa brings.
But most of all I have to thank my friends and family.
I have my family safe and sound and standing close by
To hold and comfort me.

Megan Kelly (9)
Overleigh St Mary's Primary School, Chester

Haiku

Windmill turning slow
river watching secretly
as the days go by.

> Sunset in the sky
> waiting as the days go by
> looking over Earth.

>> River flowing smooth
>> turning and bending round Earth
>> new day starts again.

Aoife Doyle (10)
Overleigh St Mary's Primary School, Chester

Haiku

Black clouds are forming
Thunder rocking and rolling
But here comes the rain.

Sam Ellams (10)
Overleigh St Mary's Primary School, Chester

The Lady Of Shalott
(Based on 'The Lady Of Shalott' by Alfred Lord Tennyson)

She looked at the knights galloping by
And people playing music on the cliff high
She looked in the mirror, then let out a sigh
And wonder'd why, o' why
              She couldn't go to Camelot!

In the market the sun shone down
On smoke from the chimneys in the town
Women in fine white gowns
              Weaved the Lady of Shalott.

Charlotte Ninnes (10)
Overleigh St Mary's Primary School, Chester

The Lady Of Shalott
(Based on 'The Lady Of Shalott' by Alfred Lord Tennyson)

The music was a sad sound,
They treasured the carpet that she wound,
And kept the boat where she was found.
They dug a hole in the ground
Right in the middle of Camelot.
Arthur placed her in the hole,
Buried her in with the rat and mole.
Lancelot then blessed her soul.
The Lady o' Shalott.

Jeremy Telford (9)
Overleigh St Mary's Primary School, Chester

Midnight Spirits - Haiku

Ghostly purple shades
Bursting through the midnight sky
Deadly spirits roam.

Samuel Garratt (9)
Overleigh St Mary's Primary School, Chester

The Lake At Dawn

Sparkling diamonds dancing on the lake
Branches curling like a slithery snake,
Spiders' webs glisten and sparkle
Dark gloomy caves as black as charcoal.

Snow-capped mountains reach for the sky,
Colourful butterflies flutter and fly.
Rising sun like a ball of fire,
Marshmallow clouds lick the tall church spire.

Along comes a man in a peaceful boat,
Looking mysterious in a long black coat.
Who is this man? Why is he here?
I am left wondering as I watch him disappear.

Beth Hallam (9)
Overleigh St Mary's Primary School, Chester

And My Heart Soars

The leaping of the dolphin,
The roaring of the tigers,,
The beauty of the stallion
Speak to me.

The sparkling of the ruby,
The sootiness of the coal,
The blueness of the sapphire
Speak to me
And my heart soars.

Louise Evans (8)
Overleigh St Mary's Primary School, Chester

Haiku

Swiftly and magic
Calm and hidden is its name
Island in the sun.

Alice Byrne (9)
Overleigh St Mary's Primary School, Chester

And My Heart Soars

The softness of the animals
The clearness of the sea
The beauty of the prayers
Speak to me.

The power of the world
The colours of the days,
The darkness of the night
Speak to me.

The work of the children,
The sparkle of the smile,
The help of the teachers
Speak to me.

Stephanie Reay (8)
Overleigh St Mary's Primary School, Chester

And My Heart Soars

The softness of the flowers,
The blueness of the sky,
The laughter of the children
Speak to me.

The saltiness of the sea,
The rustling of the leaves
The goldness of the sun
Speak to me.

Georgia Bundy (8)
Overleigh St Mary's Primary School, Chester

Haiku

Wearing all blue clothes
Cute, loving, gentle, precious
Blue eyes like the sea . . .

Demi Chelsea Tsimbilakis (9)
Overleigh St Mary's Primary School, Chester

My Own Bhagavadgita

I am the pureness of water,
I am the last sparkle in a grandparent's eye.
I am the cheeky laugh on a monkey's face,
I am the first letter in the alphabet.
I am the danger in an electric fence,
I am the fragrance in the sweetest perfume,
I am the taste in sweets,
I am the only grain of rice left in a packet.

I am the coin in a pretty purse,
I am the sound of a baby's cry.
I am the smallest tadpole in the pond,
I am the force being pulled in the stream.
I am the tickleness in a feather,
I am the sneeze from a lump of dust.

Sophie Witherstone (9)
Overleigh St Mary's Primary School, Chester

The Highwayman
(Based on 'The Highwayman' by Alfred Noyes)

Over to the inn by dawn, though Hell guards his way
The inn was lit by a candle, like the dawning of a new day
He said no word to the landlord for sure
The knights came marching, marching, marching
The knights came marching to the wretched old inn door.

Richard Grainger (10)
Overleigh St Mary's Primary School, Chester

Haiku

Immense silver moon
In the pitch-black universe
Beyond shiny stars.

Ned Pitt Knowles (9)
Overleigh St Mary's Primary School, Chester

Bhagavadgita

I am the smell of the sweetest perfume,
I am the clearness of the sea,
I am the tiredness in a parent's eye,
I am the fur on a cat's tail.
I am the scales on a goldfish,
I am the leaves on an oak tree.
I am the softness of a well-loved blanket,
I am the ink on an ancient book,
I am the laugh of a newborn baby.
I am the teeth of a fox,
I am the sparkle of the smallest star.
I am the wool of a knitted cardigan,
I am the roughness of a mountain rock.
I am the taste in a home-made cake.
I am the lead in a tiny pencil.

Rachael Alcock (9)
Overleigh St Mary's Primary School, Chester

Nowhere

Nowhere is black,
Nowhere is quiet,
Nowhere is as blank as thin air,
Nowhere is as unknown as space.
Nowhere is a bottomless hole.
Nowhere is as confusing as magic.
Nowhere is never ending.

Jack Watson (10)
Overleigh St Mary's Primary School, Chester

My Own Bhagavadgita

I am the curve in the river
I am the ink in the pen
I am the flame on the candle
I am the sourness in the lemon
I am the smoothness in the metal
I am the fragrance in the rose
I am the flight of the bird
I am the kindness in a friend
I am the roar of the lion
I am the speed of a runner
I am the fruit on a fruit tree
I am the words in a book.

Olivia Johnston (9)
Overleigh St Mary's Primary School, Chester

Nowhere

Nowhere is like a blank page,
Nowhere is dreamless.
Nowhere is unknown,
Nowhere is lost in our hearts.
Nowhere is like a room full of air,
Nowhere is hopeless,
Nowhere is unseen in the mist.
Nowhere is calm and quiet.
Nowhere is gone for ever,
Nowhere is a secret.
Nowhere is ruled by no one.

Kirsty Stubbert (9)
Overleigh St Mary's Primary School, Chester

The Highwayman
(Based on 'The Highwayman' by Alfred Noyes)

The highwayman was shattered
He loved her so.
The highwayman was on his knees,
'Please don't let me go!'

He climbed up on his saddle,
Making the horse leap,
As they both went riding . . .
Riding, riding.
'I will find her eventually, therefore she'll fall asleep.'

Sean Telford (9)
Overleigh St Mary's Primary School, Chester

My Friend

He is calm and soft
like a comfy bed and he
sticks up for me like a
meerkat protecting its group.

He is speedy as a black
jaguar. He is a bit lazy
sometimes, but the rest of
the time he's as sensible
as an owl.

Tom Inns (9)
Overleigh St Mary's Primary School, Chester

Me!

I'm active like a chimpanzee,
I'm organised like Saturday.
My stomach is as hungry as lunchtime,
I'm as bright as the summer sun.
I'm as bubbly as Fanta on the outside
And as bony as ribs on the inside.
My skin is as hot as the sun.
I'm as sleepy as a bed,
My voice is sometimes as loud as
The banging of a drum.

Lewis Smith (8)
Overleigh St Mary's Primary School, Chester

Mike

You're like autumn
mad as the wind.
You're like Saturday
wild and fun.
You're like the morning
giggly and amusing.
You're like red
a crazy lunatic.

Isaac Scott (9)
Overleigh St Mary's Primary School, Chester

My Friend

You're like winter
cold but comforting.

You're like a cheetah
fast like the wind.

You're like Sunday
calm and peaceful.

You're sunny weather
bright and reliable.

Luke Goldsmith (8)
Overleigh St Mary's Primary School, Chester

My Brother

You're like spring
peaceful and calm.

You're like a cheetah
soft but fast.

You're a sunny day,
joyful and happy.

You're the taste of tea,
warm and calming.

Alexander Benson (8)
Overleigh St Mary's Primary School, Chester

And My Heart Soars

The very clean classroom,
The refreshing water,
The interesting drawings
Speak to me.

The adventurous deep-sea diving
The barking of the dog,
The blizzard of the sands
Speak to me and my heart soars.

Anna Brodie (8)
Overleigh St Mary's Primary School, Chester

Duncan

He's red like a cherry,
Because his face fills with laughter.
He's as smart as an elephant
And never forgets anything,
Except the homework in his lunch box.
He's like the wind,
Moving on.
He's like a bee, working hard.

Joel Langmead (8)
Overleigh St Mary's Primary School, Chester

And My Heart Soars

The joy of a sunny day
The laughter of comedy
The happiness of snow,
Speak to me.

The softness of rabbits,
The friendship of my relatives.
The safeness of my home,
They speak to me
And my heart soars.

Joy Hunter (7)
Overleigh St Mary's Primary School, Chester

And My Heart Soars

The colour of the flowers,
The beauty of the mountains,
The blueness of the sky
Speak to me

The whistle of the wind,
The brightness of the sun,
The laughing of my friends.
Speak to me.

Ceri Chase (8)
Overleigh St Mary's Primary School, Chester

And My Heart Soars

The twinkling of the stars,
The softness of the air,
The colours of the rainbow.
The blazing of the sun
Speak to me.

The calling of your name,
The singing of a bird,
The tree that whistles in the breeze
Speak to me.

Olivia Brett (8)
Overleigh St Mary's Primary School, Chester

The Pied Piper

He led the children to a secret cave,
Then sat them down and played a magical tune.
He played all day until it was dark,
Then took them to a damp well,
Played a tune until the children fell asleep,
Then heard nothing but a peep.
He woke the calm children up,
Then led them back to their home
Where they lived, back in Rome.

Sophie Ferguson (9)
Overleigh St Mary's Primary School, Chester

Grandpa Bill

Grandpa Bill, Grandpa Bill,
He's like autumn but like a daffodil.
He's starting to feel elderly,
I do like Mister Will Ritchie.

Grandpa Billy, Grandpa Billy,
He's not very, very lively.
But he's like a mist quite fair
With his light, I mean white, hair.

He's like a sloth or a lion male
He's on his way to the end of the tale,
But he's still like a cushion, soft.
He's retiring into a house with no loft.

Grandpa Williams is eighty-four,
On his way to Heaven's door.
But don't cry about old Bill,
He's left me millions in his will!

Duncan Ritchie (8)
Overleigh St Mary's Primary School, Chester

The Highwayman
(Based on 'The Highwayman' by Alfred Noyes)

To the inn he rode by night, but not to be there by day.
He travelled like a speeding bullet, even tho' Hell barred his way.
He heard a shot coming from the old inn's door,
All he did was stand there thinking . . .
Thinking, thinking,
Stand there thinking, it's my fault, I just wanted more.

Joseph Hannigan (9)
Overleigh St Mary's Primary School, Chester

Miss MacSween

She's like the summer
Always shining

She's tasty
Like Margarita

She's like the cool breeze at midnight
Even when I'm sound asleep

She's like a newborn kitten
All soft and cuddly

She's like the incoming summer
All blue

She's like the soft sound of a flute
Calming.

She's like my soft duvet cover
Very friendly.

Alexandra McNee (9)
Overleigh St Mary's Primary School, Chester

Nowhere

Nowhere is a cold dull room,
Nowhere is as dark as the bottom of the sea.
Nowhere is like the middle of the Sinai desert
Nowhere is the flame from my fire.
Nowhere is like a never-ending pit.
Nowhere is my bed,
Nowhere is a mole's hole underground.

Sean Schooling (10)
Overleigh St Mary's Primary School, Chester

The Pied Piper

Everybody loves his sacred music,
But people think that he's a lunatic.
The elders follow him because they think the music is nice,
The children too and the scared mice.
The piper is a spell-caster.
People think that he's their master.
So he steps into the street
And plays five notes, so gentle and sweet.
What he wears is blue and green,
Everyone else wears yellow, pink and cream.
The Pied Piper is enchanted,
Everyone who wants a wish, it is granted.

Jake Brandon Venables (9)
Overleigh St Mary's Primary School, Chester

And My Heart Soars

The darkness of the night,
The brightness of the sand.
The giggle of the children
Speak to me.

The clearness of the sea,
The scales of the crocodile,
The softness of the clouds
Speak to me.

Jordan Chellig (7)
Overleigh St Mary's Primary School, Chester

Pied Piper

In and out of every night-like cavern,
Into a dark hole and out of the other.
All the children half a mile from their sweet home
Every one of them the spell casters to roam
Into a sapphire lake all of them splashing
Ears pricked up to the music's swift flow,
Water spluttering into the Pied Piper's pipe,
Obliterating the music like elephant to snipe,
The confused children were worried, scared as a stray kitten
They fled to the childless town to never come out,
The spellbinder tried to round them all back
He could not catch one, not even in a large swag sack,
He walked away, disappointed and sad,
His identity unknown, and that was that.

Samuel Hale (9)
Overleigh St Mary's Primary School, Chester

And My Heart Soars

The thunder of the sea,
The kindness of the fairies,
The warmness of the sun,
Speak to me.

The view of the flowers,
The freshness of the breeze.
The happiness of my family,
They speak to me and my heart soars.

Holly Pitt Knowles (8)
Overleigh St Mary's Primary School, Chester

And My Heart Soars

The petal of the flower
The colour of the rainbow
The fluffiness of the cloud
Speak to me.

The flash of the lightning
The laughing of the children
The power of the sun
Speak to me.

The panting of the dog
The tweeting of the bird
The snapping of the crocodile
They speak to me and my heart soars.

Ben Gregory (7)
Overleigh St Mary's Primary School, Chester

Snow

Crunchy, crackly snowflakes
Swish and drift through the city
Cars skid side to side behind them
Birds on their homeward journey
Peck scarlet berries off snowy bushes
Smiley snowmen shiver as they start to melt.

Niall Rogers (8)
Overleigh St Mary's Primary School, Chester

Ten Little Monkeys

Ten little monkeys hanging on a vine
One fell off and then there were nine!

Nine little monkeys arriving late
One fell over and then there were eight!

Eight little monkeys moving off to Devon
One fell off the plane and then there were seven!

Seven little monkeys performing gymnastic tricks
One fell off the bar and then there were six!

Six little monkeys performing live
One fell off the stage and then there were five.

Five little monkeys shouting for more
One fell off the chair and then there were four!

Four little monkeys playing in the sea
One ducked under and then there were three!

Three little monkeys trying to make and do
One got blotched with paint and then there were two!

Two little monkeys lifting a tonne
One fell down and then there was one!

One little monkey building a fort
He toppled over and then there was nought.

Alice Rees (7)
Overleigh St Mary's Primary School, Chester

Who Am I?

Loud barker
Tale wagger
Bone eater
Quick sleeper
Walk lover
Fence jumper.

Olivia Gough
Overleigh St Mary's Primary School, Chester

My Big Sister

You are like spring
Joyful and colourful.

You are like a tiger
Tough and safe.

You are blue
And calm as a lake.

You are like a strawberry
Sweet, but sour.

You are like a sunrise
Calm, exciting and rare.

You are like a double bed
Comfortable and soft, and big enough for everyone!

You are like Sunday
Very organised.

You are like a cat
Soft and cuddly.

You are clear
Like the sky in summer.

Molly Jones (8)
Overleigh St Mary's Primary School, Chester

Clouds - Haiku

Drifting across the
Bright blue sky, making all sorts
Of different shapes.

Like soft cotton wool
Like delicious candyfloss
Hung down from Heaven.

A fluffy fleece of
One hundred sheep, they do float
'Cross the sky above.

Sarah Thomas (10)
Overleigh St Mary's Primary School, Chester

Isaac

You are wild and windy,
Tipping off the leaves.
You are Fanta,
Fizzy and sour.
You are the morning with
The cold breeze and the glowing sunshine.
You are the alarm clock,
Waking me up with your loud ring.
You are purple,
When your cheeks blow out like a trampoline.
You are a lion
Roaring in the cage in the zoo.
You are Monday - the day is mad.
You are a breakfast bar,
Having breakfast and tea.
You are wet and windy,
So damp and steamy,
Like a bathroom.

Michael Cavendish (9)
Overleigh St Mary's Primary School, Chester

And My Heart Soars

The instruments of music
The fun that I have with my friends
The splash of the sea
Speak to me.

The books in the library
The shining of the sun
The screech of the seagull
They speak to me and my heart soars.

William Watson (7)
Overleigh St Mary's Primary School, Chester

The Beano

My favourite comic is the Beano
But my dad is such a meano.

I really think my head will burst
Because he grabs and reads it first.

I cannot bribe him with the Dandy
Or even with a glass of shandy.

I was as desperate as Dan
I had to come up with a plan.

So that we could make amends
We now decided to be friends.

And now upon our chair of leather
Me and Dad read it together.

Rhys Williams (9)
Overleigh St Mary's Primary School, Chester

And My Heart Soars

The redness of the ruby
The softness of the silk
The blazing of the fire
Speak to me.

The speed of the cheetah
The grace of the swan
The beauty of the peacock
Speak to me
And my heart soars.

Niamh Doyle (7)
Overleigh St Mary's Primary School, Chester

And My Heart Soars

The beauty of the roses
The blueness of the water
The fluffiness of the clouds
Speak to me.

The smoothness of the dolphin
The roaring of the lion
The leaping of the rabbit
Speak to me.

The laughing of the children
The chatting of the teachers
The usefulness of the helpers
Speak to me.

The chill of the winter
The blaze of the summer
The colours of the spring
Speak to me.

Emma Jones (8)
Overleigh St Mary's Primary School, Chester

And My Heart Soars

The laughter of the children
The beauty of the flowers
The softness of the pillows
The softness of the clay
Speak to me.

The beauty of the sun
The softness of a baby
The softness of your hair
Speak to me.

Charles Tice (7)
Overleigh St Mary's Primary School, Chester

And My Heart Soars

The laughing of the children
The lightness of the starlight
The sweetness of the grass
Speak to me.

The blueness of the sky
The softness of the clouds
The voices of the angels
Speak to me.

The sound of the birds
The footsteps of the ants
The roaring of the sea
Speak to me.

Melissa Jones (8)
Overleigh St Mary's Primary School, Chester

And My Heart Soars

The saltiness of the sea
The glory of the Earth
The sparkle of the stars
Speak to me.

The sparkling of the Saviour
The hotness of the sun
The darkness of the sky
Speak to me and my heart soars.

Lucy Clegg (8)
Overleigh St Mary's Primary School, Chester

Football Crazy

Football here we come
But I can't play because I am dumb
When I score a goal
My foot goes down a hole
And when I kick the ball
I fall flat on the floor
Then I get a stitch
When I am running down the pitch
And when I am in goal
My face hits the pole.

Meg Rawlinson (10)
Overleigh St Mary's Primary School, Chester

And My Heart Soars

The saltiness of the sea
The singing of the birds
The firmness of the rock
Speak to me.

The slowness of the tortoise
The freshness of the air
The quacking of the duck
Speak to me.

Callum Gough (7)
Overleigh St Mary's Primary School, Chester

The Oak Tree

An oak tree
Sprouted from a tiny sapling
Tall, grand, mighty
Like a tall, stately king whispering in the wind
Like a ladder reaching to the clouds
Makes me feel small and vulnerable
Like a droopy flower waiting to be crushed
An oak tree
Makes us realise how much we do not know.

Mary Scott (11)
Overleigh St Mary's Primary School, Chester

Me

I am as bright as the summer sun
I am as fizzy as Fanta and chewy as chicken
My stomach is as hungry as lunchtime
I am as stripy as a tiger on the outside
And as soft as a kitten on the inside
My feet are as crinkly as the blue sea
I am calm like a Sunday
I am the banging of a drum
I am as soft as a bed
I am hot like the sun.

Tom Batten (9)
Overleigh St Mary's Primary School, Chester

And My Heart Soars

The size and width of the world
The brightness of the sun
The gushing of water
Speak to me.

The greenness of the grass
The friendship of my friends
The redness of the autumn trees
They speak to me and my heart soars.

Christopher McCartney (7)
Overleigh St Mary's Primary School, Chester

And My Heart Soars

The shining of the sun
The sound of the animals
The swaying of the trees
They speak to me.

The softness of the sand
The colours of the rainbow
The chatting of the people
They speak to me.

Mollie McIlwaine (7)
Overleigh St Mary's Primary School, Chester

Moon - Haiku

The gold crescent moon
Drifts across the sky till dawn
The stars catch its light.

Harry Redmayne (9)
Overleigh St Mary's Primary School, Chester

The Scuttling Arachnid

Spinning its silky web
Delicate, breakable, fragile
Like a hunter setting a trap
Like a fisherman hauling in his catch
Giving me inspiration to persevere
Like Robert the Bruce in the cave
Scuttling . . .
A macabre attic full of cobwebs.

Peter Young (11)
Overleigh St Mary's Primary School, Chester

My Friend

You are just like the summer
Bright and open.

You're like a truck horn
Big and loud.

You are dark as midnight
But as close as a brother.

Jake Parry (9)
Overleigh St Mary's Primary School, Chester

Beth

You're like the sun, shining brightly
You're always happy
Like the colour yellow.

You're like the TV
Like a bright, new day.

You're spicy and sometimes blush.

Molly Degg (8)
Overleigh St Mary's Primary School, Chester

If

(Based on 'If' by Rudyard Kipling)

If you can go to work with people
who don't understand your troubles . . .
If you can keep your cool when people
make a joke out of you . . .
If you can keep going to school even though
it's hard to live at home . . .
If you can concentrate on your work when
there is something else always on your mind . . .
If you can do what you know is right
without being asked . . .
If you stand up for the right and talk the truth . . .
If you help a sad person who also feels
like there's a shadow hanging over them . . .
Then you will be a person that little children can look up to!

Chris Ratcliffe (10)
St James' CE School, Clitheroe

A Firework

Like a rocket shooting up into the sky,
coloured like a rainbow,
sounds like we're saying goodbye,
sparkling like diamonds and rubies,
never stops glistening,
shooting up like a plant,
growing like a flower.
They make a bundle of laughter and joy
and fill our hearts with brightness.

Victoria Jackson (8)
St James' CE School, Clitheroe

If . . . Then . . . What?
(Based on 'If' by Rudyard Kipling)

If you went for a whole day without talking,
If you were not to speak just once,
If you counted all the steps you've taken,
If you have taken over one thousand,
If you went for a whole day without getting told off at school,
If you didn't get told off once . . .

If you could run around the school without getting told off,
If you could believe in any religion,
If you could not hurt yourself,
If you could be friends with everyone,
If you could have longer break times . . .
Then . . . then . . . what?

Emma Hook (11)
St James' CE School, Clitheroe

The Sun

Like . . . hmm . . .
A fiery hot fireball staying in its place,
A spiky-rimmed hat,
A flying saucer,
A big bowl of custard not being eaten
And feeling like a lot of fire.

Linda Sou (8)
St James' CE School, Clitheroe

The Sun

Like . . . hmm . . .

As yellow as custard,
As round as a football,
As bright as a light,
As hot as an oven.

Lauren Ross (8)
St James' CE School, Clitheroe

If . . . Then . . . What?
(Based on 'If' by Rudyard Kipling)

If you did not talk
If you did not walk around
If you did what you were told
If you lived a life with no pain
If you had real friends . . .

If you could save lives
If the animals on the wall were red
If the sun shone all day
If you worked and worked
If you worked with everyone . . .

If you did all this
You would be the happiest
Man/woman on Earth.

Jodi Novak (11)
St James' CE School, Clitheroe

A Storm Cloud

Like . . . hmm . . .
a fluffy dark pillow
a mummy getting angry with her kids
a dark shadow that blocks the sun
as black as the midnight sky
a bubbly Aero.

Kirby Robinson (9)
St James' CE School, Clitheroe

If . . . Then . . . What?
(Based on 'If' by Rudyard Kipling)

If school was so easy,
If school was no fun,
If school was so strict,
It wouldn't be fun.

If school had no playtimes,
If school had no colour,
If school had no good cooks,
Then school meals would be yuck!

If school had no pictures,
If school had bare walls,
If school had strict teachers,
Then nothing would go on.

If school had no PE,
If school had no laughing,
If school had a long day,
Then . . . then . . . what?

Zoë Clayton (10)
St James' CE School, Clitheroe

Tree Poem

Like . . . hmm . . .
A tall person who hasn't cut his nails.
Like a giant who is always standing in the same place.
Like a giant prickly snake.
A statue of a prehistoric tree.
A person's hair that hasn't been combed.

Mark Faulkner (8)
St James' CE School, Clitheroe

If . . . Then . . . What . . . ?
(Based on 'If' by Rudyard Kipling)

If you are good at maths
If you are good at English
If you are good at history
If you are good at geography
If you are good at science
Then . . .

If you are good at cleaning up cuts
If you are good at staying up late
If you are good at helping people
If you are good at sorting things out
If you are good at being calm
Then . . .

If you are good at standing in the cold
If you are good with computers
If you are good with people
If you are good at playing an instrument
If you are good at singing
Then . . .

If you are good at cooking
If you are good at talking for a long time
If you are a kind person
If you are funny
If you are good at writing a lot

Then . . . you will be a good teacher!

Lauren Barton (10)
St James' CE School, Clitheroe

The Sun

As hot as a ball of fire.
As yellow as a bowl of custard.
As bright as a shining light.

Natasha Watson (9)
St James' CE School, Clitheroe

If . . . Then . . . What . . . ?
(Based on 'If' by Rudyard Kipling)

If you play every day . . .
If you play on a computer all day . . .
If you boast to your friends . . .
If you are rubbish at PE . . .
If you like school meals . . .

If you can rule the school . . .
If you can sing great . . .
If you shout something bad . . .

Then you will play for a top team
Then you'll get square eyes
Then you'll lose friends
Then you'll be good at maths
Then you'll get extra chips

Then you'll be headmaster
Then you'll be in a opera
Then you'll go to the headmaster.

Jake Nuttall (10)
St James' CE School, Clitheroe

The Sun

As hot as a ball of fire
As yellow as a bowl of custard
As bright as a shining light
As round as a football.

Jack Dewhurst (8)
St James' CE School, Clitheroe

If
(Based on 'If' by Rudyard Kipling)

If you can copy from a French dictionary for one hour, and finish it . . .
If you can do all your work on the computer and never get caught . . .
If you can go into assembly with no school uniform and hide behind other people . . .
If you can hear a rumour about your friend, but never spread it . . .
If you know all the answers to the questions, but never get asked to answer them . . .
If you get everything right, but you never get praised or thanked . . .
If you can understand the work you've been given, but manage to be the only person to listen in a crowd . . .
If your best friend hurts your feelings but you always forgive them . . .
If you follow the good and ignore the bad, when the time's right . . .

Then you will follow God's commandments and always do what's best!

Ellie Tolson (10)
St James' CE School, Clitheroe

If . . . Then . . . What . . . ?
(Based on 'If' by Rudyard Kipling)

If you could do all your work with the same pen . . .
If you could throw your rubber and not get told off . . .
If you could snap a ruler and not get found out . . .
If you could do good work without putting your hand up . . .
If you could do PE without running . . .

You'd be the perfect pupil!

Joshua Mansfield (10)
St James' CE School, Clitheroe

A Tree

Like . . . hmm . . .
Like a statue standing very still.
Like a person standing still waving their arms.
Like a big nest with a stand.
Like a soldier standing still because the Queen is coming.
Like a fountain with its arms as its tubes that the water comes from.
It stands like a giant.
Like a girl with bushy hair.
Like a goalkeeper trying to save a goal.
When the wind blows the arms look as if they are slashing
                                            other trees down.

Katie Moss (9)
St James' CE School, Clitheroe

A Tree Poem

Like . . . hmm . . .
Standing like a big fat giant stuck in the ground,
like a big flower that is not very pretty and doesn't smell
very nice.
Big long fingers that are rotting and in the autumn
the long nails fall off.
The leaves are like a big green Smartie.
The truck is like a big brown chocolate bar.
A statue stuck in the long grass.
A person's hair that is uncombed.
Sounds like a waterfall splashing all over everything.

Charli Charnley (9)
St James' CE School, Clitheroe

If

(Based on 'If' by Rudyard Kipling)

If you work hard at school all through your school life . . .
If your hand never goes down in class . . .
If you can ignore horrible insults . . .
If you can study hard at home and at school . . .
If you don't retaliate to bullies who try to annoy you . . .
If you can obey a teacher's command . . .
If you don't fidget in class at all . . .
If you can be polite to everybody . . .
If you always try to improve your work . . .
If you are always on time for school . . .
If you are committed to school . . .
If you always hand in your homework . . .
If you are helpful in every way . . .

You will be happy all your school life!

Jack Knowles (10)
St James' CE School, Clitheroe

Sun

The sun is like . . . hmm . . .
A golden corner on the cob
A football
A bonfire with its embers burning
A buttercup dancing in the grass
Happy children playing in the park.

Luke Gregson (9)
St James' CE School, Clitheroe

If
(Based on 'If' by Rudyard Kipling)

If you can go into assembly and sit for hours with a ramrod-straight back . . .
If you can keep your hand in the air all day without even getting asked one question . . .
If you can get all your own kit into your PE bag and not end up with two left plimsoles . . .
If you can be clean and good all week . . .
If you can be quiet all day . . .
If you can do all your work and get it right . . .
If you can finish that story . . .
If you can stay out of a fight and not get involved . . .

Then you are a star!

Rebecca Dixon (11)
St James' CE School, Clitheroe

If
(Based on 'If' by Rudyard Kipling)

If you can go through a day listening to your teachers . . .
If you can go through a day answering questions . . .
If you can remember your PE kit every week . . .
If you do not get distracted in your work . . .
If you hear a rumour and do not spread it . . .

If you can do all of this then you will be rewarded with team points!

Liam Nuttall (11)
St James' CE School, Clitheroe

If

(Based on 'If' by Rudyard Kipling)

If you could listen to the teacher and not get bored . . .
If you could be bad and be let off . . .
If you could talk all day and not get done . . .

If you could do whatever you wanted . . .
If you could be a teacher all day . . .

If you could play outside all day . . .
If you got no homework . . .
If you had art all day . . .

Then school would be truly great!

Bethany Tomlinson (11)
St James' CE School, Clitheroe

Fireworks

Fireworks are like . . . hmm . . .
A trigger of a gun being pulled,
Someone drawing on the sky,
Everyone is watching them,
They can be every single colour in the world,
They are just as colourful as a rainbow.

Jake Place (9)
St James' CE School, Clitheroe

Fire . . .

Is a very hot oven,
Is a yellow flower,
Is an asteroid on the ground,
Is a Venus flytrap ready to strike at any time.

Robert Hembury (9)
St James' CE School, Clitheroe

I'm A Little Pussy Cat

I'm a little pussy cat sitting in a tree,
eating mushy bananas and an enormous green pea.

I'm a leapy seal sitting on some rocks,
with a friend as a fish who gives me lots of socks.

I'm a brown rabbit in a hole,
trying to get out with my big long pole.

I'm a pink flamingo with short legs,
I like eating yummy scrummy eggs.

Victoria Rose (8)
St James' CE School, Clitheroe

The Sun

A bowl of custard.
As hot as a fire.
A big, sparkling yellow ball.
As hot as a cooker on fire.
As bright as a sunflower.
As bright as a yellow metre stick.
As bright as a literacy book.

Aimee Neild (8)
St James' CE School, Clitheroe

The Sun

Like a bright stack of sweetcorn,
Like a football in the sky,
As hot as a bonfire,
Like a sunny buttercup,
As bright as a yellow metre stick.

Shannon Braithwaite (9)
St James' CE School, Clitheroe

Treasure Under The Deep Blue Sea

D iving under the sea is fun
E very day I find some treasure
E ven some people find it a pleasure
P earl necklaces in the box

B lue dolphins swimming round the box
L ovely fish with them
U nder the box there's more treasure
E mpty shells floating around

S and covering all the box
E xciting things are under the box
A ll is exciting under the sea.

Jessamy Britcliffe (7)
St James' CE School, Clitheroe

Animals Everywhere

One cross pelican sitting on a rock.
Two nasty rats playing with some hats.
Three chattering parrots eating a little carrot.
Four tired tigers eating some toast.
Five cute kittens find some mittens.
Six ugly puppies playing with some trucks.
Seven speckled horses eating some leaves.
Eight squeaky dolphins eating lots of fish.
Nine pink flamingos playing bingo.
Ten stomping elephants playing with their friends.

Kirsten Hunt (8)
St James' CE School, Clitheroe

If . . . Then . . . What?
(Based on 'If' by Rudyard Kipling)

If we did all the work
If we didn't get told off
If we didn't talk when we were not meant to
Then we might get a team point.

If we get on with each other
If we stick together
If we work as a team
Then we will be unbeatable!

Jordan Rose (11)
St James' CE School, Clitheroe

The Breakfast Poem

When I was munching an egg
a monster popped out with a hairy leg
he was covered in yolk
and nearly got eaten by a stork
then helped himself to my cup of tea
went to the fridge to get a pea
then fell in my cup of tea
then he had a piece of toast
and dried himself on the morning post.

Jack Ryan (7)
St James' CE School, Clitheroe

School

S chools are good,
C lass is silly,
H ow do teachers go so chilly?
O ur head teacher is so mad,
O ur teacher is so sad,
L ovely children listen, so bad!

Natalie Bristol (8)
St James' CE School, Clitheroe

If
(Based on 'If' by Rudyard Kipling)

If you do all your work . . .
If you are prepared for every lesson every day . . .
If you can help your teacher all day . . .
If you remember your PE kit all the time . . .
If you are polite and helpful . . .
If you can get all your own PE kit into your PE bag
                and not end up with two left pumps . . .
If you aren't nasty to your friends . . .
If you do all your work right . . .
If you listen all the time . . .

Then you will achieve all your golden time!

Laura-Jane O'Neil (11)
St James' CE School, Clitheroe

If
(Based on 'If' by Rudyard Kipling)

If you walk away from a fight . . .
If you can get your coat without it being on the floor . . .
If you can put your hand up for ten minutes . . .
If you do your homework and bring it in the day after . . .
If you do not talk all day.
If you win a race . . .
If you bring your PE kit in . . .
If you play football without getting told off . . .

Then you will be a better person!

Emily Aspinall (10)
St James' CE School, Clitheroe

If
(Based on 'If' by Rudyard Kipling)

If you can go into assembly and sit for hours with a
ramrod-straight back . . .
If you can keep your head in the air all day long without
even getting asked one question . . .
If you can get all your kit back into your PE bag and not end up
with two left plimsoles . . .
If you can do your work in one minute and not move down ten minutes
on golden time . . .
If you can get one thousand team points and not get stopped
in the middle . . .
If you love football but cannot play it for a day,
then can you take it?

Sarah Anne Margaret Davies (11)
St James' CE School, Clitheroe

If
(Based on 'If' by Rudyard Kipling)

If you can hear a rumour and not spread it . . .
If you can think a silly thing but not say it out loud . . .
If you can sit and work without a word spoken . . .
If other people go on the computer while you read, without
groaning . . .
If you can dance and never speak of badness . . .
If you can play football and never speak of gladness . . .
If you can help a fallen body who has been hurt, lonely
and sobbing . . .
If you can do all these things you will become an all-new king.

Christopher O'Reilly (10)
St James' CE School, Clitheroe

If
(Based on 'If' by Rudyard Kipling)

If you can go into assembly and sit for hours with a
ramrod-straight back . . .
If you can keep your hand in the air all day without
even being asked one question . . .
If you can get all your own kit back into your PE bag
and not end up with two left pumps . . .
If you can be nice and kind all day and not get mad . . .
If you can do all your work and get it right . . .
If you can try all day not to get in a fight . . .
If you can be good all day and not get your teacher mad . . .

Then you will be rewarded!

Tyler Spencer (11)
St James' CE School, Clitheroe

I Don't Care

Try to scare me, I don't care, even though it's not fair.
Clean my windows, I don't care, even though it's not fair.
Turn the TV on, I don't care, even though it's not fair.
Shout real loud, I don't care, even though it's not fair.
Do all those things, I'm asleep in a deep, deep sleep.
You can do them, definitely more than a peep.

Reece Monk (7)
St James' CE School, Clitheroe

If
(Based on 'If' by Rudyard Kipling)

If I can go to school and listen . . .
If I can hear a rumour and not pass it on . . .
If I can be called names and not call someone something back . . .
If I can write a poem . . .

Then I will be a happy boy!

Jeremy Piercy (10)
St James' CE School, Clitheroe

If
(Based on 'If' by Rudyard Kipling)

If you can hear a rumour and not spread it . . .
If you don't shout out and put your hand up . . .
If you can work well without talking . . .
If you can write neatly and not make one mistake . . .
If you can bring your PE kit in and not borrow someone else's . . .
If someone falls over and you help them up . . .
If you can walk away from a fight without hitting someone . . .
If you complete your targets and finish your book . . .

Then you will be rewarded with prizes!

Ben Rose (11)
St James' CE School, Clitheroe

If
(Based on 'If' by Rudyard Kipling)

If you can listen to the teacher for six hours and not fall asleep . . .
If you can sit up in class all day and not talk . . .
If you can go for your bag and not find that something is missing . . .
If you can get your lunch and find it's not burnt . . .
If you can play outside and stay away from the fights . . .

Then you can be a better person!

Poppy Johns (10)
St James' CE School, Clitheroe

Molly The Dog

M olly the dog
O wners think she's a mutt
L ots of treats she gets
L ots of training
Y eti she looks like. In snow you can't see her.

Melissa Cox (9)
St James' CE School, Clitheroe

If . . . Then . . . What . . . ?
(Based on 'If' by Rudyard Kipling)

If you can write all day and not finish the title . . .
If you can do PE all day and not sweat . . .
If you can do a thousand lessons of woodwork and not
                                      get a splinter . . .
If you can sing every song word-perfect . . .
If you can stay in every playtime yet not be bad . . .

If you can get every sum right without a calculator, paper or brain . . .
If you can sit straight-backed for hours on end . . .
If you can escape and come back the next second . . .
If you can do schoolwork easily . . .
If you can make the school a better place . . .

Then, if you want to be, you're the teacher!

Adam Johnson (10)
St James' CE School, Clitheroe

If
(Based on 'If' by Rudyard Kipling)

If you can be good and not talk . . .
If you keep asking someone something all day and not lose
your patience . . .
If someone falls over and you help them up and let them
join in a game . . .
If school is bad and everyone else has been bad . . .
If you listen to the teacher and get on with your work . . .

Then you will go far in life!

Wesleigh Russell (11)
St James' CE School, Clitheroe

If . . . Then . . . What . . . ?
(Based on 'If' by Rudyard Kipling)

If someone is nasty, then upset someone else.
If you forget your pencil case then buy another.
If your water spills all over the table, then clean it up
If children throw books all over the place then Miss Leeming
                                                  clears them up.
If someone pulls your bobble out and then drops it on the floor.
If you get a team point taken off for crying then get another
                                                  from talking.

If everything was about 'If' the world would have ended by now.

Amber Townley (10)
St James' CE School, Clitheroe

If
(Based on 'If' by Rudyard Kipling)

If you can go into assembly without talking . . .
If you can listen all day without talking . . .
If you know a secret without telling anyone . . .
If you can keep all of your work neat and tidy . . .
Then you should be good all of the time.

Lindsay Roberts (11)
St James' CE School, Clitheroe

If
(Based on 'If' by Rudyard Kipling)

If you can think hard all day and not talk . . .
If you can walk away from a fight . . .
If you do not fight all the time . . .
If you cannot do something but try your hardest at it . . .

Then you will not lose golden time!

Tom McBride (11)
St James' CE School, Clitheroe

If . . . Then . . . What?
(Based on 'If' by Rudyard Kipling)

If you could sneak someone's secret sweet supply
                               but not be caught . . .
If you could never listen to what you are being taught . . .
If you could hide in the staffroom and not be found . . .
If you could bury your maths deep in the ground . . .
Then what . . . ?

If you could answer every single problem and sum . . .
If you could always be best and number one . . .
If you could bring an apple in for the head . . .
If you could finish your SATS and not be dead . . .

Then all I can say is you should be in bed!

Naomi White (10)
St James' CE School, Clitheroe

Houses

H umid in summer weather
O ur house is horrible
U gly paintings on cream walls
S oapy water in the sink
E gg sandwiches in lunchboxes
S illy children in the bedroom.

Matthew Johnston (7)
St James' CE School, Clitheroe

The Sun

As hot as an inferno
As yellow as a yellow Smartie
As big as a yellow Earth
As hot as a fire phoenix
As hot as a fire that you cannot put out.

Aron Stevenson (9)
St James' CE School, Clitheroe

Happy Days

H appy days, they're real good fun.
A t last the night has passed, the day has come.
P arents happy, me happy, what a day it's gonna be!
P eople happy, me happy, what a day it's gonna be!
Y o dude! A good day it will be, I'm gonna jump up and down
                                                            with glee.

D ays, beautiful days, a brilliant day it will be.
A t last the day's gone through, it's time for bed
Y o! It's bed for you too!
S o then a new day it is, what a great day it will be.

Henri Webber (10)
St James' CE School, Clitheroe

I Can See

I can see a bed on my head.
I can see a tie in a pie.
I can see a car near a bar.
I can see a pea near a bee.
I can see a sky way up high.
I can see a cat looking fat.

Levi Barnes (7)
St James' CE School, Clitheroe

Raining

It's raining
I don't like the rain
When the sunshine is out
I can go outside and sing and shout
But when it's raining
I have to stay inside.

Paige Bithell (7)
St James' CE School, Clitheroe

If . . . Then . . . What . . . ?
(Based on 'If' by Rudyard Kipling)

If you can stay at school without talking,
If you don't stop at school they will send you walking,
If you tell over someone they won't be your friend.
If you steal something you won't be able to lend.
If you say naughty words, you get sent out,
If you don't be nice, you can get shouted at.
If you're not good at something try, try again,
And if you put dynamite in the school and blow it up
You will be put in custody.

Sam Townsend (11)
St James' CE School, Clitheroe

Coronation Street

Monday night at 7.30,
There is a double episode.
I think I will explode.
Grab the crisps and the drink,
I don't want to blink.
Here it comes, It's on, *ssshhh*,
It's started!

Ilona-Jade Worsley (9)
St James' CE School, Clitheroe

School

S chool is good, it makes me laugh and play
C lass is cheerful on one beautiful day
H ow I love school
O h, it's so much fun
O h I love it here, I'm
L oving it at St James' School.

Amber Barnes (7)
St James' CE School, Clitheroe

If . . . Then . . . What . . . ?
(Based on 'If' by Rudyard Kipling)

If you snap a pencil, then sharpen it.
If your teacher shouts at you say, 'Sorry.'
If you don't write your title, write it.
If you're getting bullied, just punch them.
If you break a pen, pay for it.
If someone is sad, play with them.

If you do all these things, you're a good person.

Paul Coward (11)
St James' CE School, Clitheroe

The Playground

Down the slide,
It's a slippery ride.
Play on the swing,
It's like you have wings.
On the roundabout,
If you want to get off, *shout!*
On the climbing frame,
Hurry up, it might rain.

Rhian Melvin (9)
St James' CE School, Clitheroe

The Teacher From Leeds

There once was a teacher from Leeds
who swallowed a packet of seeds.
In less than an hour,
her nose was a flower
and her hair was a bundle of weeds.

Cian Lee (9)
St James' CE School, Clitheroe

Seasons

Summer is hot,
But winter is not
And autumn is just in the middle,
Spring is fine,
I rate it at nine
Because summer is much more fine.
I see no leaves in winter,
But they will start to grow a little later,
In summer the leaves will have grown
And in autumn sometimes the leaves fall alone.
In summer I lick ice cream,
In winter I taste the turkey,
So that's how I feel about the seasons,
So remember which season comes next!

Helen Sou (9)
St James' CE School, Clitheroe

Hamster

H ow cute
A little furry face
M istake, chewing on my lace
S taring with dotted eyes
T hey're very small in size
E veryone likes it
R ight, that's my hamster.

Hannah Marshall (10)
St James' CE School, Clitheroe

If . . . Then . . . What . . . ?
(Based on 'If' by Rudyard Kipling)

If you could shout
Across the classroom and not get grassed on . . .
If you could lob a rubber
At the teacher and not get sent out . . .
If you could be a person
With a scruffy hairdo and never get bullied . . .
If you could get away with anything
And do all that things that you wanted to . . .
If you could send notes
And not listen to Madam French
And if you could do no work
And be at your ease all day . . .

Then it would be
A miracle!

Billie-Jo Jackson (11)
St James' CE School, Clitheroe

A Cat

A cat is like . . . hmm . . .
Two ice creams dropped on the ground,
Like a teacher with whiskers and ears,
Maybe a carrot, but better,
Or a planet with a nose.

Emma Fosberry (8)
St James' CE School, Clitheroe

If . . . Then . . . What . . . ?
(Based on 'If' by Rudyard Kipling)

If you did not speak for a day . . .
If you did not fall out . . .
If you did not be late for school . . .
If you did not write for so long . . .
If you did not be naughty . . .
If you did not have a bad hair day . . .
If you did not moan and groan . . .
If you did not bully lots of people . . .

Then you would have a good day!

Dean Gordon (10)
St James' CE School, Clitheroe

Winter

W inter is the best season of the year,
 I t isn't like autumn with nothing to do.
N o, in winter you can do anything,
T o see snowballs just appear from nowhere,
E verlasting mugs of hot chocolate,
R ocking chairs creaking in front of the television.
T he snow is freezing unless you've got gloves on.
 I n their houses people playing board games.
M any people asleep after a great day's play.
E verybody likes winter, it's the best season of all.

Callum Dickinson (9)
St John's CEP School, Nelson

Winter

W inter is breezy.
I ce is cold.
N elson is frozen.
T ime to play out.
E verybody is playing and having lots of fun!
R olling in snowflakes.
T he snow is cold!
I cy snowmen with black hats on.
M ums turning up the fire.
E verybody wants to stay in and keep warm.

Philippa Dinsdale (9)
St John's CEP School, Nelson

Winter

W inter is here again,
I ce cream too cold now,
N ights are very dark and cold,
T rees are swaying about,
E very time I get up it is snowing,
R ain splashes on rooftops.
T ime to wrap up warm,
I gloos, some people are building them now,
M ums are throwing snowballs at you,
E verybody is cold.

Scarlett Kinsella (9)
St John's CEP School, Nelson

Winter

W intertime, snow and winds that blow.
I ce-aged lakes and snow-hung trees.
N ot very warm but very bitter.
T he winter winds are getting stronger.
E venings are getting longer and longer.
R iding down hills in my sledge.
T he days of winter are getting wilder.
I n the house we watch the trees tilt.
M y hat keeps blowing into the trees.
E verybody playing and making snowmen.

Luke Parkinson (9)
St John's CEP School, Nelson

Winter

W inter is here
I cy flakes are hanging from my roof
N ice cold times are here again
T rees are covered in snow
E veryone is enjoying the snow
R obins are putting their heads under their wings

D angers, icy flakes are hanging from my roof
A nd lots of snow too
Y ummy tea and cocoa is being made.
S nowmen are being built.

Usman Arif (9)
St John's CEP School, Nelson

Winter

W inter is cold,
I like to keep warm,
N elson is icy,
T he ground is covered in snow.
E verybody building snowmen,
R ush to the fire to keep warm.
T he snow is great to sledge in,
I love to throw snowballs.
M ums want us to keep warm,
E verybody wants to stop in bed.

Aaron Hirst (10)
St John's CEP School, Nelson

Winter

W inter's wonderful,
I t is amazing,
N o sun, all snow,
T all trees blow,
E verybody's cold.
R obin Redbreast sits on the tree.
T oo cold for outdoor swimming,
I cicles hang from the roof,
M ake snowmen,
E verything's white.

Anthony Denney (9)
St John's CEP School, Nelson

Winter

W hen the snow falls from the sky,
I cicles hang from the windows,
N ice warm nights sitting by the fire,
T rees are covered with snow,
E veryone is making snowmen,
R obins with their red chests.
T he windows are covered in frost,
I gloos are everywhere,
M ugs of cocoa warm us up,
E veryone enjoys this.

Richard Bailey (9)
St John's CEP School, Nelson

Spring

S pringtime is coming,
P ink flowers are growing.
R oosters are going in the fields,
I n all the sun.
N ewborn calves are coming,
G oing to need plenty of milk.

D ays are getting longer,
A nimals are coming out of hibernation,
Y ou can now pick flowers in the sun,
S pringtime is coming.

Katherine Illingworth (9)
St John's CEP School, Nelson

Fright In The Night

I feel a fright in the night,
yes, that's right,
in the night.
Yes, that's right,
I hold my covers
tight, tight, tight!

I hear a thud in the night,
yes, that's right,
in the night,
and hope it doesn't
bite, bite, bite!

Oh, that night I did have a fright,
that night I was left with *a-a-a-a-a*
       fright!

Lauren Atherton (10)
St Thomas' CE Primary School, Leigh

My Grandma

Wears clean glasses when she reads,
Her dark green eyes are as green as grass,
Greying hair,
And has a warm, welcome smile.
She is short and small,
Cracking crosswords are her favourite,
Likes to read the newsy newspaper.

Laura Mulcahy (9)
St Thomas' CE Primary School, Leigh

In The Jungle

In the jungle
I hear a noise!
What can it be
A monkey, a baboon
Or a chimpanzee?
I sit and watch
Waiting and wondering
If it will leap at me.

In the jungle
I hear a noise!
A rustling of leaves
Or maybe a lion's sneeze
I have a look around
To see what is there
But guess what?
It isn't a bear.

In the jungle
I hear a noise!
But what can it be this time?
I hear it again
Twice
Surprise, surprise!
Out they all come
Roaring and hissing
Singing and whistling.

I hear a noise
But not in the jungle this time
In my dream!
In my dream!

Bethany Cook (10)
St Thomas' CE Primary School, Leigh

My Favourite Foods

M ine to control,
Y ou cannot have it.

F ried eggs and fish,
A crispy food,
V ery delicious and precious,
O h how I love my favourite foods,
U ncle Ben's rice,
R avioli,
I love them all,
T urkey and chips,
E ggs, toast, bacon and sausages,

F ried toast,
O h, yum, yum, yum!
O ranges and octopus,
D onuts, lick your lips,
S o what's your favourite food . . . can I have it?

Phillip Whitehead (10)
St Thomas' CE Primary School, Leigh

Colours

Red is for a roaring fire on a winter night,
Or Manchester United's football kit,
It could be a poppy on Remembrance Day,
Or a bottle of red wine.

Blue could be a swimming pool,
Or the angry sea,
It's the colour of our school jumper,
Or the bright blue sky.

Callum Leyland (10)
St Thomas' CE Primary School, Leigh

Playground Poets

P is for poets as writeful as can be.
L is for laughing when we talk.
A is for amazing games we play.
Y is for yapping when we chat a lot.
G is for ground that we play on.
R is for run when we race.
O is for ordinary poetry lessons.
U is for us when we play.
N is for nurse with sharp needles.
D is for dinner at 12 o'clock.

P is for playing at playtime.
O is for occasional arguments that we have.
E is for entering this competition.
T is for teaching, that's what our teacher does.
S is for singing in the playground.

Rebecca Healey (9)
St Thomas' CE Primary School, Leigh

Two Weeks Of Fun

Chattering children
Sketch slowly
While standing on the bank
Paint going everywhere
Make a mistake, Bryan's magic cloth dissolves the mistake
Man comes in and takes a picture, everyone's happy
And in the newspaper
Last day with Bryan, the fun is now over.

Kelliejo Colbert (9)
St Thomas' CE Primary School, Leigh

My Best Friend

M ine, mine, mine, my best friend
Y ou make me laugh, you make me happy.

B rilliant you are
E ven though we fall out, we're still best friends
S uper, super, super best friends
T hat's all you are to me.

F riendship is important to us
R acing home to play
I ce cream, we both love
E xactly, we're best friends
N aughty we can be
D eep, deep down, we are best friends.

Matthew Lambert (11)
St Thomas' CE Primary School, Leigh

A Wet, Windy Day

Cold, wet, muddy on the canal,
Me wrapped up all nice and warm,
Boats zooming past,
Ducks go 'Quack, quack.'
Swans with their beautiful white silk feathers,
People going past on bikes,
Looking at lovely warm, cosy houses,
Oh, I wish I could go back.

Lauren English-Rowland (9)
St Thomas' CE Primary School, Leigh

Sketching

A cold Monday afternoon walking along the path.
Excited, freezing, as the wind blew our hair
Sketching time had come at last
And I'm really proud of my drawing.

Heather Morris (9)
St Thomas' CE Primary School, Leigh

Why Bother With SATs

SATs are boring.
SATs are bad.
When I do SATs they make me go mad.
But they could be good for later life,
When you have a job and maybe a wife.
When I finish them I feel happy.
Then I get my results, that's when I feel really unhappy.
But then again, they're not that bad.
It's not like I'm going to cheat off Brad.

Sam Rowlands (10)
St Thomas' CE Primary School, Leigh

Brilliant Bryan

Brilliant Bryan sketching slowly and carefully,
Brainy Bryan does outstanding pictures outside,
                               sketching all the time,
Silly students have to listen to what boasting Bryan has to say,
Brilliant Bryan helps us to sketch speedily,
Brilliant Bryan helps us to paint pretty pictures.

Rayyah Unsworth (9)
St Thomas' CE Primary School, Leigh

Painting

Paintbrush, Paintbrush
Slap it on the paper
Splish, splash, splosh
All wet and gooey
As the soggy paint
Drips down the board.

Paige Briscoe (9)
St Thomas' CE Primary School, Leigh

Colours

Orange is a fire blazing,
Sun in the sky,
Or a fox prowling about woods,
A juicy fruit that you eat.

White is for the snow falling gently,
Sparkling teeth in your mouth,
Or doves flying,
Clouds, fluffy as can be.

Red is for roses growing everywhere,
Apples, ready to eat,
Or juicy strawberries,
Poppies remembering people.

Helen Slater (10)
St Thomas' CE Primary School, Leigh

Painting

Splish, splash, splosh,
I sway and swerve my brush,
Mixing magical colours,
Bright blue, dark blue,
Pretending to stroke the cat,
Isn't painting fun?

Kirstin Houghton (9)
St Thomas' CE Primary School, Leigh

Dirty!

Wrapped up warm,
I was off!
Deep, dark and dismal canal,
Walked along looking at litter.
Why was the canal so dirty?
Sketched the bridge,
Came across graffiti.
Really cold,
Drew graffiti.
Horrible,
Shivering,
Sank in the mud.
Sky, miserable and cloudy.
So cold, lips turning blue.

Chloé Yates (9)
St Thomas' CE Primary School, Leigh

Boys!

B is for boys, horrible and silly!
O is for obey, which boys never do!
Y is for yawning which boys do in lessons!
S is for stupid and silly, that's what boys are like!

    Boys! Boys! Boys!
        Who on the Earth
            Wants them?

Lucy Mellan (10)
St Thomas' CE Primary School, Leigh

The Big Challenge

Chilly children sketch outside,
They take their pointy pencils,
With their creative clipboards,
Bryan accompanies them.
Inside, warm children do pretty paintings,
Stroke paintings with the colours brick-brown and sky-blue.
Painting with bristled brushes.
How wonderful to see all magical mixed colours
It looks beautiful now it's finished.
    The fun is over!

Ashley Pritchard (9)
St Thomas' CE Primary School, Leigh

Colours

Green

Green, the colour of a dirty swamp
Or a sly crocodile snapping its teeth,
New fresh leaves and cows munching the juicy grass.

Blue

Blue, the nice clear sky
Or ink waiting to be used
And dolphins splashing in the ocean,
The deep, dark sea.

Heather Garfin (9)
St Thomas' CE Primary School, Leigh

Here's A Clue

There is something in the kitchen that I bought for you!
But don't guess, I'll give you a clue,
Its wrappers are in a pattern of purple and blue,
Have you guessed yet, here is another clue,
It's a creation, a sensation, needs no concentration,
It has gone through the nations with its temptation,
Have you guessed yet, here is another clue,
It comes in all shapes,
It comes in all sizes,
I wanted it but I had to be wise,
I couldn't find the right one,
I didn't find the wrong one,
I wanted one,
I wanted two,
For now it awaits you!

Jessica Bridget Anderson (11)
St Thomas' CE Primary School, Leigh

My Dad

The laughing boss of the house,
Cute, tough and strong,
Helps me with my homework,
Makes the house gleam,
Cheers for Liverpool on the telly,
Enters the house with a smile,
I can't imagine what it would be like without him,
Of all the dads in the world, I'm happy that he's mine.

Amy Boardman (9)
St Thomas' CE Primary School, Leigh

My Alien Family

My mum has two eyes of lead
on the top of her head.
She's got a job to pose
as she has a really long nose.

Me, well I'm practically perfect in every way,
I go to school in the Milky Way.
I've got a level 4A,
and a level 4B,
that's me.

My brother, he's great,
he's only eight,
to me he's nutty,
for a lot of footy.

My gran is old,
she's always cold,
she's always blue,
she's not like me or you.
She's out of this world, anyway, your world.

Stephanie Boardman (10)
St Thomas' CE Primary School, Leigh

The Day We Sketched With Bryan

It is cold as we are sketching Mather Lane Bridge.
Paint perfect pictures.
Brilliant Bryan helps us.
Splish, splash, as we paint the pictures.
Bryan paints perfect pictures on boards.

Abigail O'Brien (9)
St Thomas' CE Primary School, Leigh

Alphabet Poem

A is for angry ant
B is for bendy banana
C is for cool car
D is for dumping dog
E is for eating eggs
F is for forgetful fish
G is for grumpy goat
H is for hungry hippo
I is for ice-cold ice lollies
J is for jiggly jelly
K is for karate kangaroo
L is for local lobster
M is for missing monkey
N is for nameless newt
O is for objecting octopus
P is for possessed polar
Q is for quiet queen
R is for rude rabbit
S is for savage snake
T is for tidy table
U is for uniting unicorn
V is for vain vulture
W is for worrying water
X is for Xmas X-ray
Y is for yapping yo-yo
Z is for zipping zebra.

Gemma Stockley (10)
St Thomas' CE Primary School, Leigh

Walking

Walking is lovely
No people drinking bubbly
Crunching leaves at your feet
No nasty, fatty meat.

Marching, everybody clapping
Nobody shopping
The boots go dashing
Nobody clashing.

Jogging in the lane
Nothing plain
Burning off the calories
Better than everybody's salaries.

Simon Lowe (9)
St Thomas' CE Primary School, Leigh

The Painting

Chattering children paint peacefully,
Brilliant Bryan is the local artist,
Bryan is friendly, fun and kind,
Boasting Bryan paints perfectly,
All the colours, yellow and red,
We mix the colours to make more instead,
Perfect painting finishes fabulously.

Shelby Harris (9)
St Thomas' CE Primary School, Leigh

The Colour Poem

Red
Red is paint dripping down a wall,
Or a juicy apple hanging off a tree.
Could be a mouth-watering drink of red wine,
Or a big blazing fire on a log.

Blue
Blue appears to be water running down a mountain,
Could be a breeze sweeping through the air,
Or the Earth moving around the atmosphere,
Hearing the ocean's roar.

Black
Black is the night sky,
Or the tar on the ground,
And a tuxedo,
The colour of people's shoes.

Green
Green is the colour of healthy grass,
Or a swamp,
The colour of sprouts,
And the colour of a crocodile.

Yellow
Yellow is the colour of hot custard,
Or a sunflower,
Could be leaves,
Or a yellow crayon.

Adam Wilkes (10)
St Thomas' CE Primary School, Leigh

Last Night's Football Game

Last night Arsenal played Man U
Arsenal played absolutely bad
Man U won 4-2
But Arsenal played absolutely mad.

First goal by Patrick Vieira just inside the post
Hope that is one at the most
Then Giggs pulled one back
Giggs gave it one hell of a smack!

Then a goal came back, Dennis Bergkamp under the legs
They call it nutmegs
At half-time, 2-1 down,
Man U came on with a frown!

Craig Town (9)
St Thomas' CE Primary School, Leigh

Dolphins

D is for dolphins that swim in the sea
O is for octopuses that swim underneath
L is for laughing, that's what dolphins do
P is for peeping that they do on the surf
H is for hyperactive for when they are giddy
I is for ice which is sometimes near
N is for naughty which the dolphins are sometimes
S is for sneaky because the dolphins are.

Anna Woodburn (9)
St Thomas' CE Primary School, Leigh

The School Nurse

The school nurse is coming,
She walks in humming.
There's dread in the air,
But I don't care
If the school nurse is coming.

The school nurse calls me forward,
She thinks I'm a coward.
There's dread in the air,
But I don't care
As the school nurse calls me forward.

The school nurse roots in my hair,
Will she find nits in there?
There's dread in the air,
And I do care
If she finds nits in my hair.

Hope Gill-Daintith (10)
St Thomas' CE Primary School, Leigh

Colours

Red
Red is a blazing flame alone in a field
Or a planet like Mars so far away
Red is the colour of blood when you cut yourself
Or a great big juicy apple hanging from a tree.

Blue
Blue is the colour of the rain falling from the sky
Or one of the beautiful colours of the rainbow
Blue is the colour of a tear falling off a face
Or the beautiful sky above.

Paul Burke (10)
St Thomas' CE Primary School, Leigh

Stars

Stars twinkle in the sky
Stars don't make me cry
Stars gleam in the night
Don't let them give you a fright.

Stars gleam brighter than white
The stars white flow so bright
Stars twinkle, twinkle in the night
They want me to take a flight.

Stars sometimes have to go,
So sometimes I shout, 'No!'
The moon appears in the sky
Then I go to fly.

Clare Aikin (8)
St Thomas' CE Primary School, Leigh

The Cold Wet Canal

Cold, wet and muddy on the canal,
Freezing pupils sketch eagerly on the giant bridge,
Sploshy paint drips on the massive board,
Muttering children chattering to genius Bryan.
The amazing cloth wipes off all the horrible mistakes,
Oh I wish he could come back!

Jack Morris (9)
St Thomas' CE Primary School, Leigh

Dolphins

Dolphins, dolphins in the sea
Dolphins, dolphins jump at me
Dolphins, dolphins play with me
Dolphins, dolphins smile at me

Dolphins, dolphins sing with me
Dolphins, dolphins look at me
Dolphins, dolphins swim with me
Dolphins, dolphins dance with me

Dolphins, dolphins I found you
Dolphins, dolphins I love you
Dolphins, dolphins play with me
Dolphins, dolphins in the sea

Dolphins, dolphins look at me
Dolphins, dolphins smile at me
Dolphins, dolphins I smile back
Dolphins, dolphins say goodbye.

Amy Knowles (8)
St Thomas' CE Primary School, Leigh

Dogs

My dog, my dog ran into a wall
My dog, my dog ran into a car
My dog, my dog ran into a lamppost
My dog, my dog goes to sleep.

My dog, my dog sometimes bites
My dog, my dog has walks with me
My dog, my dog plays with me
My dog, my dog sleeps with me.

My dog, my dog ran into a wall
My dog, my dog ran into a car
My dog, my dog ran into a lamp post
My dog, my dog goes to sleep.

McCauley Collier (8)
St Thomas' CE Primary School, Leigh

The Rat And The Cat

The rat and the cat just go munch,
Also together every lunch.

They both go to the dock,
Just to stock a stupid clock.

Across the field lives a flea,
They always have some stew for tea.

I don't know what to sell,
How about a doorbell?

Now we must travel along,
Can we ring a dinner gong?

What could be at the stall?
We are so terribly small.

Now it's time to say goodbye,
Do you want a piece of pie?

Darren Jackson (9)
St Thomas' CE Primary School, Leigh

Fighting Soldier

Children getting evacuated,
Bombs are exploding,
Aeroplanes getting blown up,
Soldiers go into the dens,
Soldiers feel scared,
Planes flying in the sky,
Dropping bombs from the sky.
Mums working in the factories.

Lisa Billington (11)
St Thomas' CE Primary School, Leigh

Weather

The sun is fun
The moon has a tune
The clouds are like crowds
The sky can fly
The air plays fair
The rain is the same
The hurricane is lame
The gale is pale
The snow does its show
The ice is nice
The sea is like me
The hailstone does moan
The mist can twist
The fog has a pet dog
The tornado has some play dough
The breeze can tease
The frost can pay the cost.

Lewis Birkbeck (8)
St Thomas' CE Primary School, Leigh

The Soldier In The War

I can see big bombs floating in the air
and planes firing in the sky.
I can feel rain down my back,
my feet are cold and wet.

I am missing my family and my friends.

I can hear the sound of rain on the ground
and I can hear the bombs banging all around.

Bethany Taylor (10)
St Thomas' CE Primary School, Leigh

Summer, Summer

Summer, summer, having ice cream.
Summer, summer, into the pool.
Summer, summer, flowers grow.
Summer, summer, play outside.

>Summer
>Summer
>Summer.

Summer, summer, going on holiday.
Summer, summer, having fun.
Summer, summer, it is good.
Summer, summer, it is hot.

>Holiday
>Holiday
>Holiday.

Summer, summer, having a picnic.
Summer, summer, playing on bikes.
Summer, summer, having a tan.

>Tan
>Tan
>Tan.

Joanna Morris (8)
St Thomas' CE Primary School, Leigh

The Soldier

I could see planes bombing us.
The soldiers took cover,
They dug deeper and deeper by the minute,
It was cold and painful.
The bombs were exploding.
In the dangerous night dark fell
On soldiers hungry and with aching feet.

Rebecca Brighton (10)
St Thomas' CE Primary School, Leigh

Alphabet Poem

A is for Amy who is a lady
B is for Bart who is apart
C is for Carol who is a barrel
D is for Den who is a pen
E is for Ellie who is a nelly
F is for Fred who loves his head
G is for Graham who hates playing
H is for Hailey who loves Bailey
I is for Ian who hates Liam
J is for Joanna who loves her spanner
K is for Kelly who loves her belly
L is for Liam who hates Ian
M is for Mikita who loves Peter
N is for Nicole who loves marshmallow
O is for Olive who loves porridge
P is for Peter who loves Mikita
Q is for Queenie who loves her bikini
R is for Rhys who looks like the police
S is for Sandra who looks like a panda
I is for Thomas who looks like a promise
U is for Umar who looks like a star
V is for Violet who is a pilot
W is for Wendy who is bendy
X is for Xerxes who is a Mavis
Y is for Yvonne who is strong
Z is for Zack who is a yak!

Ruby Taylor (8)
St Thomas' CE Primary School, Leigh

Man Utd Match Days

Man United are the best
They will be a great test
They will win away
Whenever you say.

Man United has the best players
Their pitch is full of layers
Ronaldo is a joy on the wing
As the fans sing

Man United are winning two-nil
The away manager is taking a pill
Sir Alex Ferguson is chewing gum
The away fans want their mums

The goalkeeper catches the ball
Because he's very tall
He kicks it upfield
Through the defence shield

Man United win and the match is over
Somebody is driving away in a Rover
The away fans are going to the shop
To get a brand new Man United top!

Zack Uzokwe (8)
St Thomas' CE Primary School, Leigh

Soldier

The soldiers are fighting for their wives and their children.
I can hear bombs exploding and people crying.
I can hear planes overhead and it is scary.
Bright bombs are exploding in the sky.
I feel scared because people are crying at night.
I feel lonely and sad.

Jodie Kniveton (10)
St Thomas' CE Primary School, Leigh

All Mixed Up!

Cats are doing backflips,
Umbrellas for the wind.
Boys wearing clips,
Everyone's being sinned!

People flying around,
Nothing's normal here.
Nobody on the ground,
Except Dad drinking beer!

Kids eating ice cubes,
In the snow.
The slides are tubes,
Mountains are very low!

This town is all mixed up!
Get me out of here.
I'll fly away in a cup,
When I'm home, I'm going to cheer!

Jessica Unsworth (8)
St Thomas' CE Primary School, Leigh

The Soldiers

I can see bombs exploding,
people fighting for their lives
and people huddling together.

Bombs exploding,
shooting here and there,
and roaring planes coming past
and soldiers crying for their lives.

I feel sad for my family,
and I have sludge right up to my heels
and I am cold.
The rain is dripping down my nose
and neck and I am scared!

James Stuart Massey (9)
St Thomas' CE Primary School, Leigh

A Box

I open my presents,
And what do I see?
A box of surprises;
Treats for my birthday, all shapes and sizes.

I ignore the surprises
Inside the boxes,
I like the outside more.
What can I do with it?

An aeroplane, a car, a train;
What can I make?
A house, a boat and a trampoline.
Have I made it?

What can I make out of this thing?
An imaginary mind,
This box is the home for me,
And my imaginary mind.

Lauren Oakes (10)
St Thomas' CE Primary School, Leigh

A Soldier In The War

I can see bombs in the sky and on the ground.
I can see people crying for help.
I can see children, families and friends.
I can see the brave army stamping around.
I can hear mummies and daddies saying their goodbyes.
I can feel myself afraid of death.
I can feel my heart break.

Ashley Pavitt (9)
St Thomas' CE Primary School, Leigh

Daydream

I'm in my racing car shooting across the ground,
I'm going so fast I can't hear a sound,
I'm going round a turn, look out, help, *smash!*
I've hit my dad, *ow!* What a crash.

I am a captain sailing the seven seas,
My ship is sailing gently in the breeze,
I can see my mum baking a cake,
Sailing makes you hungry, time for a break!

I am a doctor, operating now,
How I'm going to save this guy, I don't know how.
Here comes my dog, 'Down, boy, down!'
He's wiping mud all over my gown!

I'm a pilot, I'm flying through the air,
The force of the wind is pulling back my hair,
Help, a missile is coming! 'Dive!'
It's just a cap gun fired by my brother Clive!

Adam Williams (11)
St Thomas' CE Primary School, Leigh

Me In The Way

I can see children being evacuated from their mums and dads.
Some of them are saying that they don't know where they are going.

I can hear children crying for their mums and dads
who are crying for them too.

I can feel people pushing me and prodding me and I feel so sad
because I am leaving my children all on their own.

I can hear machine guns shooting people and trying to shoot
the people who are killing people, so I get my gun out and start
to shoot.

I can see bombs exploding in the sky, people trying to save
other people's lives.

Bayley Swinburn (9)
St Thomas' CE Primary School, Leigh

My Cardboard Box

I am a hunter in my cardboard box,
I'll get my gun ready, here comes an ox,
I get down and aim at its head,
It falls on top of me and now I am dead!

I am a spaceman in my cardboard box,
Blasting aliens with great big spots,
Walking on the moon is so much fun.
It is great now the fun has begun.

I am an athlete in my cardboard box,
Running fast in my lucky red socks,
Jumping hurdles is so exciting,
It's time for our results, it is so, so frightening!

I am a pilot in my cardboard box,
Blowing up aeroplanes, people and docks,
Flying past the ocean at 100 miles an hour,
Now I am flying past Blackpool tower.

Here is the end of our great big ride,
This is my last chance to say goodbye.

Sam Boydell (10)
St Thomas' CE Primary School, Leigh

War Has Started

The soldiers sail across the sea with their little lanterns.
The guns' bullets shoot into the sky like lightning.
I can hear planes shooting across the sea and machine
                                                    guns vibrating.
Next the men are marching across the bridge.
The soldiers also hear bombs explode in their ears.
I can hear the bricks crashing.

Paul Turner (9)
St Thomas' CE Primary School, Leigh

My Imagination

Boats are a-swaying in the bath,
Cats and dogs dancing on the path.
Lions and tigers, the fight has begun,
Using your imagination is so much fun.

Princes and princesses falling in love,
Angels and fairies fly up above.
Bathing and swimming deep in the sea,
A gold-haired mermaid is playing with me.

Driving the carpet through the cold wind,
Now it's the time for fun to begin.
Driving past valleys, mountains and trees,
Dragons and snakes are bothering me.

Playing with blocks and knocking them down,
Turning my smile into a frown.
It's time for bed now, it's 9 o'clock,
Saying goodbye to the boats on the dock.

Rebecca Lowe (11)
St Thomas' CE Primary School, Leigh

War

I can see aeroplanes flying in the air ready to bomb us.
I can hear bombs exploding in the night and the planes
flying overhead in the sky.
I'm feeling that I am missing my wife and little children
and my mates and family.

I am very lonely and scared of the bombs exploding in the city
and the houses getting bombed.

Jamie Taylor (9)
St Thomas' CE Primary School, Leigh

Princess Belle School Fairground Ride

I am a schoolgirl sitting out there,
Having fun playing on the fair
Round we go, up as well,
All of a sudden I become Princess Belle.

Long brown hair, flashy dress
With a puff of smoke I become Princess Jess.

My father with one golden crown
Said to me, 'I am so proud of you
Being princess of the town!'

Then there's my mum,
Sunbathing in the sun,
Wearing her hair in a big fat bun.

Jessica Mathews (11)
St Thomas' CE Primary School, Leigh

The Tumbling Spaceship

What can I play with a duvet and pillow?
I'll pull it off my bed and my duvet will billow,
Then I lie it flat on the floor.
I climb inside, my pillow as my door.

I roll through my room like a bird in the air,
I get to the landing, I'm nearly there.
I stop for a rest, my heart's beating fast;
I peep through the door and hear a big blast!

I'm tumbling, tumbling down the stairs,
I might die, so *beware!*
I'm at the bottom, I'm still alive,
Mars will have to wait till I'm five.

Jenny Goodison (11)
St Thomas' CE Primary School, Leigh

Who Am I?

I'm a creature,
Swimming through the sea,
Not even a shark
Could surely catch me?

I've got a tail,
Lovely and gold,
My friend is a dolphin,
With skin so cold!

I'm only pretending,
Don't worry about me,
Guess who I am!
Who could I be?

I've got pretty and long,
Sparkly hair,
Guess who I am,
If you *dare!*

I am a mermaid!
Did you know?
I can hear the school bell,
I really must go!

I hope you enjoyed
Playing with me.
Imagination is as easy as
1, 2, 3!

Natalie Hilton (10)
St Thomas' CE Primary School, Leigh

A Little Spy

When I was little
I was Tom Cruise
Looking for a bomb
Inside my mum's shoes.

Spying on neighbours
From my high chair
Having a row,
Pulling each other's hair.

Under my bed
I made a base,
Hanging from a skyscraper
Secured with a lace.

But now all my dreams have disappeared,
Now I look in the mirror
I can see . . .
Some grey in my beard.

Jack Castledine (10)
St Thomas' CE Primary School, Leigh

Little Sisters

Little sisters are boring
Because they're always snoring
The sunlight makes me happy
But makes my sister poo in her nappy.

When I come to clean it up
She would have wiped it on our pup
So I got her dressed
But she's still a pest.

So I came to say
That's the end of the day
I am very glad
Because I would have gone mad.

Jemma Bentham (8)
St Thomas' CE Primary School, Leigh

The Houses Bombed Down

I can see the aeroplanes
dropping bombs and missiles.

I can hear the siren going off
and machine guns firing
and I can hear an army marching
along the muddy surface
and I can hear footsteps squelching
and squishing.

The other people are sad around me
and I feel sad and scared and
I feel lonely to leave my home and my family.

I can see bombs landing and
houses knocked down in half.
All the people want is a safe place.

Anthony Smith (10)
St Thomas' CE Primary School, Leigh

I Am A Soldier Fighting In The War

I am a soldier fighting in the war
I can see bombs going off all over the place,
Lighting up the dark and dangerous night sky.
Planes soaring through the night.
Soldiers tired and hurt.
I can hear the machine guns going off all over the place,
The engines of the planes above.
The sounds of the bombs exploding above my head.
I am feeling very, very sad because I am missing my family
                                                and friends.
I am scared because I do not know if I might be killed.

Sylvia Clayton (11)
St Thomas' CE Primary School, Leigh

My Wonderful Imagination

Nearly time to play out,
Please start thinking but don't shout!
Has anyone thought of a game,
Because I'm sick of the same?

I've thought of a game,
It's called wonder and fame.
It's just my imagination
But then I take my medication.

Ring, ring, there goes the bell,
I ran quickly but down I fell.
I picked up my bag and ran to the hall,
I imagined I was running from the ball.

Now I'm at home,
I feel all alone,
I go to bed
With dreams in my head.

Jenna Stevenson (11)
St Thomas' CE Primary School, Leigh

Soldier

I can see a soldier fighting
I can her a soldier saying,
'Come on, because we need to fight!'
I feel upset because I am missing my family.
I can see something in the sky.
It is a plane!

Matthew Naughton (11)
St Thomas' CE Primary School, Leigh

Something's Stirring!

Deep, deep down in the cellar,
There's a man named Stella
He is a *killer!*
His wife is Cilla
Something's stirring,
    Something's stirring.

In a deep dark corner,
There is Sauna,
The ghost of our story,
This is the glory.
Something's stirring,
    Something's stirring.

In the middle of the room
There is doom, doom, doom.
Someone's shaking
This is breaking.
Something's stirring,
    Something's stirring.

Something's stirring in the cellar,
But we don't know what it is,
And it's coming . . .
    Something's coming.

In a year or two it's back,
Gobbling up the people,
Nothing's stirring,
    Nothing's stirring.

Lucy Taberner (9)
St Thomas' CE Primary School, Leigh

Summer

Summer, summer, having ice cream
Summer, summer, in the swimming pool
Summer, summer lazing around on the beach
Sitting on a deckchair.

Summer
Summer
Summer

Holidays, holidays
I'm not going peach
I'm going brown!

Dogs running round the beach,
Crabs nipping people's toes on the beach
People laying around in the deckchairs

Fish in the sea
Dolphins in the sea
Whales in the sea

Holidays, holidays
I'm not going peach
I'm going brown.

Emma Taberner (8)
St Thomas' CE Primary School, Leigh

Cold And Chilly

Cold and chilly sitting on the bank
Sketching the mill
Ducks swimming past
Litter floating by taking to time
Next day out again and sketching
The church this time.

Molly Newport (9)
St Thomas' CE Primary School, Leigh

Days Of The Week - Alliteration

On Sunday, Sam the snake was watching the sun shine.
On Monday, Matthew the monkey was eating bananas and
                                                   saw a mouse.
On Tuesday, Tilly the tortoise ate some Twizzlers.
On Wednesday, Willy the wizard waved his wand at a witch.
On Thursday, Tufty was thirsty and thinking.
On Friday, Fiery Fred had a film.
On Saturday, Sally the Sindy doll had a friend.

Abbie Cox (7)
St Thomas' CE Primary School, Leigh

Days Of The Week - Alliteration

On Sunday Sam the snake ate some slime.
On Monday Martin made mischief all day.
On Tuesday Timmy Turner tasted some Twizzlers for tea.
On Wednesday Wilma went to get some wood.
On Thursday I thought of a theatre.
On Friday my father had a fried egg.
On Saturday I listened to a song.

Matthew Taylor (7)
St Thomas' CE Primary School, Leigh

Days Of The Week - Alliteration

On Sunday Sam the snail went to the seaside.
On Monday Mister Mankey went to the market.
On Tuesday Angel tried to catch a toy.
On Wednesday Wilma was a wizard.
On Thursday there were thoughtless thieves.
On Friday I caught four fish.
On Saturday Sam sat on a sofa.

Harry Thompson (8)
St Thomas' CE Primary School, Leigh

Days Of The Week - Alliteration

On Sunday Sammy swapped sandals.
On Monday Molly the monkey got up to mischief.
On Tuesday Tim told Tom to watch Tommy on TV.
On Wednesday Wilma walked on water.
On Thursday I thought I was three.
On Friday I thought the film was funny.
On Saturday Sandy went to a swimming party on a swan.

Katie Unsworth (8)
St Thomas' CE Primary School, Leigh

Days Of The Week - Alliteration

On Sunday Sammy and Simon swam at the seaside.
On Monday Mrs Monkey made some maths.
On Tuesday Thomas took a treat.
On Wednesday Walter went on a walk.
On Thursday the thinking monster threatened.
On Friday I found my friend, Mrs Francis.
On Saturday I saw a spider spinning a web.

James Pickles (7)
St Thomas' CE Primary School, Leigh

Days Of The Week - Alliteration

On Sunday Sally saw a sunflower.
On Monday Molly made mischief.
On Tuesday Tim tickled my tum.
On Wednesday I went to Woolworths.
On Thursday I thought of things.
On Friday I fried a fish.
On Saturday I sat on a seed.

Kirsty Anderton (9)
St Thomas' CE Primary School, Leigh

Days Of The Week - Alliteration

On Sunday Sammy the snail was asleep in his shell.
On Monday Mark the monkey was up to mischief.
On Tuesday Tina and Timmy were talking times tables.
On Wednesday Wilma was wide awake.
On Thursday thirty thunders were there.
On Friday Fred and Fran were there.
On Saturday Sammy was on the swings.

Jilly Westhead (7)
St Thomas' CE Primary School, Leigh

Days Of The Week - Alliteration

On Sunday Sammy the slug shone in the sun.
On Monday Melly the monkey got up to mischief.
On Tuesday Tim the tiger tried to trick the tortoise.
On Wednesday Weasel the wheel went wild.
On Thursday the three thin aliens thought they could think.
On Friday Mr Frightening fell forward in the field.
On Saturday Sam shone his shoes.

Adam Oakes (7)
St Thomas' CE Primary School, Leigh

Days Of The Week - Alliteration

On Sunday Sammy the snail smiled at the sun.
On Monday Molly the monkey got up to mischief.
On Tuesday Tim the tiny teddy tried to tap a tulip.
On Wednesday Willy Wellington went to watch a whale.
On Thursday you thought of good things.
On Friday Mrs Francis met my friends.
On Saturday I smiled at the sun.

Katie Hickson (7)
St Thomas' CE Primary School, Leigh

Days Of The Week - Alliteration

On Sunday Sammy went to the seaside
On Monday my mum married a man
On Tuesday the top of my toe was tickling
On Wednesday the weather was warm
On Thursday the thunder was threatening
On Friday the fish was frightened
On Saturday the sun was shining.

Leah Burke (8)
St Thomas' CE Primary School, Leigh

Days Of The Week - Alliteration

On Sunday Sam the slug slimed around.
On Monday Mr Monkey met a mouse.
On Tuesday Timmy the toad talked.
On Wednesday Willy went to the wizard.
On Thursday thirty monsters counted to three.
On Friday Freddie the freak went to sleep
On Saturday Sammy the slug went to sleep.

Bethany Sharrock (7)
St Thomas' CE Primary School, Leigh

Days Of The Week - Alliteration

On Sunday Sam sat on the grass to watch the sun shine.
On Monday Molly the monkey dropped some milk.
On Tuesday Tommy told me things.
On Wednesday Willy the whiz walked with the witch.
On Thursday Tom thought things.
On Friday four friends followed me.
On Saturday six singin' sweet swans sung.

Lauren Smith (9)
St Thomas' CE Primary School, Leigh

Scary Mary!

There was once a girl called Mary,
We thought she was rather *scary*
She had a jet-black cat,
She had named the cat Rat.
What a weird name it is, I have to say,
But saying this, so was Mary!

She would never ever, ever share,
We were all very scared.
She shouted at us in the playground,
We were frightened of the sound.
Mary made us all run away,
When we asked if we could play.

One day we realised she wasn't there,
Where did she go? No one knows where.
Some people say she ran away,
Some people say she moved to Leigh.

Still who knows where she went?
Nobody cared, they weren't her friend.
She moved away, she had some time
To change herself from nasty to kind.

She arrived back at the school,
Mary was friends with everyone in her classroom.
Everybody liked Mary,
She was now 'friendly Mary'!

Siobhan Ryan (10)
St Thomas' CE Primary School, Leigh

My Dog (Smudge)

Smudge has a long hairy tail,
He has furry, brown paws.
With a grey-white head.
His tummy is black and curly,
Which is very cuddly.
He's got white sparkling teeth,
With great big fangs.
Smudge has got a calm bark,
His whiskers tickle all down my face.
He loves to scrap and play.
As well he might seem sweet and cute,
But he scratches me all the time.

My dog is the best.

Bethany Robinson (10)
St Thomas' CE Primary School, Leigh

Recycle, Not Litter

Recycle for the world,
Even candy wrappers swirled.
Plastic bottles,
Bottle tops
And if your litter really drops,
You may get caught by the cops.
If you recycle,
You might help a life-cycle.
So just think before you litter,
That your soul knows it's wrong.
Just remember in your head, this little poem song,
Now then, recycling, that's not wrong.

Marnie Bickett (9)
St Thomas' CE Primary School, Leigh

Late

Every morning 8 till 9
I'm wasting my own time.
Waiting outside,
I want to hide.
The head is my fright
Yes, that's right!
The head gives me a fright.

He's waiting outside,
He knows I'll hide.
Letting the teachers guard the other gate,
I definitely have no mate
To help me escape.
To get me through the gate.
The teacher is my fright,
Yes that's right!
The teacher gives me a fright.

And that day the school inspector comes,
And we all stand and sneer.
He doesn't look hard
But he looks a little bit mard.
He goes around to every class,
Looking through the window glass.
They all are my fright,
Yes that's right!
They all give me a fright.

Jennel Anne Kalyan Unsworth (10)
St Thomas' CE Primary School, Leigh

I Hate School!

I hate school,
Playing out: cool.
Lessons: bad.
Silly old Dad,
Late for school,
I love swimming pools
School unlucky,
Chickens are clucky
I hate school,
Home time now.
Getting in my swimming pool!
Yeah!

Emma Kennerly (11)
St Thomas' CE Primary School, Leigh

I Want shoes

I want shoes,
Red, blue, white or black,
Multicoloured in fact.

I want shoes,
Boots, trainers or heels,
Sandles in fact.

I want shoes,
Happy, sad or in the blues,
I want shoes
What size are you?
'Cause I'm size twos!

Alison Meeson (10)
St Thomas' CE Primary School, Leigh

Playground

P is for playing with a skipping rope
L is for listening to each other
A is for the amazing games we play
Y is for yawning, which we do at the end of the day
G is for the ground which we play on
R is for the races which some of us win
O is for occasional arguments we have
U is for U and me sitting on the bench
N is for nice, the way we play
D is for dances we showed each other today.

Jessica Marsh (9)
St Thomas' CE Primary School, Leigh

Colours

Blue is the uniform which I wear
Or a bluebell with a lovely scent,
Maybe rain dripping on my head and
Puddles on the ground, wet and cold.

Yellow is the colour of sunshine drifting
Across the sky,
Lightning crashing to Earth.
Butter melting on my hot toast,
Lemons sour and tarty, it makes my tongue
Go funny.

Catherine Buckley (10)
St Thomas' CE Primary School, Leigh

What I Saw . . .

Warm and cosy
Sketching places
Vandalism all around
Smashed windows
Trees and swans
Graffiti on walls
Factories and houses
Litter and rubbish
In the canal
But I enjoyed it all.

Kerry Linley (9)
St Thomas' CE Primary School, Leigh

My Brother AJ

AJ my brother is called
Only three
Has a big happy smile
Naughty, sometimes though
Very kind as well
Indeed he's very cute
He's got very short hair
Not a freckle on his face,
Has his own way of being jolly.

Nicole Pendlebury (10)
St Thomas' CE Primary School, Leigh

Spring-Heeled Jack

Green Dragon Alley was cold
Green Dragon Alley was dark
In the stinking streets of London
The dark city air
The mixture of mud and rubbish
Spring-heeled Jack
Spring-heeled Jack.

Peckham prowler puzzles police
Out of their senses
This deranged man
The flickering orange light
A Peckham resident
Spring-heeled Jack
Spring-heeled Jack.

Wearing shining armour
Hackney as a lamplighter
Slithered on the cobbles
Off into the mist
You'll freeze to death
Spring-heeled Jack
Spring-heeled Jack.

Paige Mary-Louise Jackson (10)
Shavington Primary School, Crewe

I Am The Girl

My name is Jessica Lea Youle
I am the girl who sculptured the world,
I glistened the sunset yellow and orange.
I created the sky so blue, so I could
See the birds that flew.
The flowers are white, purple and lilac
So I could see them through the green grass.
I moulded the rainbow for it to play
With the blue sky on a rainy day.
I am the girl who sculptured the world.

Jessica Lea Youle (11)
Shavington Primary School, Crewe

The World I Made For You

My name is Miss Hope Laura Jean,
I am the girl who painted and sculptured the world.
I shaded the grass green, so it could sway beautifully with the breeze,
I created the wind so it would blow in your face.
I crafted the soil to give a home to all the bugs, slugs and snails,
    I carved the world just for you.

My name is Miss Hope Laura Jean,
I am the girl who designed the world with colour,
I created butterflies to high up hopes,
I crafted the rainbow to lead a path to the sky.
I designed the moon to leave a trail in the night,
I shaded the grass green, so it could sway in the breeze,
I made the seasons to have a change of time,
    I sculptured the world just for you.

Hope Kurzawa (10)
Shavington Primary School, Crewe

Hate

I am as old as the first person to argue,
I was born in the blackness of people's spirits.
My brothers are Sadness and Anger,
I wear a shroud of blackness to cover me completely,
I live in the very darkest thoughts ever,
My ambition will be to take over Love and Happiness.
My fear is living in the likes of Happiness.
My greatest success is to defeat world Happiness.

Jamie Millington (11)
Shavington Primary School, Crewe

Enough To Make You Sick!

What if every day you ate,
Food of twice your body weight?
This is what *some* people want to do!
Think what it would mean to you . . .

Seven bucketful's of chips,
Several dozen instant whips,
Twenty packs of Shredded Wheat,
Thirty tins of luncheon meat.
Is this what you'd want to eat?

Plus - six chickens and a ham,
Forty-seven pots of jam.
Fifty bars of Milky Way,
All that in a single day.
Lovely! did I hear you say?

Pea green soup, nice and thick,
Is this enough to make you sick?
Or would you rather be a stick?

Francesca Wilkinson (11)
Shavington Primary School, Crewe

Hate

My name is Hate.
I have a brother, Evil,
And two sisters, Anger and Death.
I live in Hell with orange,
Red and yellow flames around me.
My greatest ambition is
To make everyone live in pain
And cry every day.
My biggest fear is to be happy.

Lydia Oakley (10)
Shavington Primary School, Crewe

The World I Made For You

My name is Olivia Charlotte Jackson,
I am the girl who created the seasons for a change every 3 months.
The sculptured rocks were created so the seagulls had a home,
I crafted the glass rainbows, so they glistened always.
I moulded every little grain of sand so it could blow freely,
                                            in the howling wind,
I am the creator of these things.

My name is Olivia Charlotte Jackson,
I fashioned the lilies into colours like pink, purple and white,
I created the sunset in amber, yellow and rouge
                                        to make relaxing evenings,
I designed the fluffy marshmallow clouds so the sky had a friend,
I carved the old oak trees so the roots were a friend to the worms.
I created these things just for *you!*

Olivia Jackson (11)
Shavington Primary School, Crewe

Mother Nature

My name is Daniel John Simon,
I am the boy who designed the sea,
I squeezed the blue into the open sea,
I made it so wet that only fish can survive,
I crafted the stars to shine all night long,
I carved the oak trees to become king of the forest,
I moulded them together so the leaves had somewhere to live.

My name is Daniel John Simon,
I created the sunset to show my moon and stars off.
I fashioned the sunset to make the sky look beautiful,
I invented humans to keep the animals company,
I freely made humans to enjoy the sea,
I did all of that for you!

Daniel Simon (10)
Shavington Primary School, Crewe

A Poem Of Nature

My name is Laura Jayne Vickers,
I am the girl who splashed blue to the sky
So it wouldn't complain about being dull.
I created the clouds all fluffy and white,
So the sky would not be lonely.
I designed butterflies to bring colour into the world.
I glistened the stars into the sky at night
So the moon could have some friends.

My name is Miss Laura Jayne Vickers,
I am the girl who sploshed water to make the sea
So fish could live their happy lives there.
I carved the trees so they could talk to each other
As the day passes through.
I moulded the soil to enable worms to wriggle in the dirt.

I did this all for you.

Laura Vickers (11)
Shavington Primary School, Crewe

I Made The World

My name is Tom David Atkinson,
I am the boy who splashed red into roses to make them bright,
I carved the butterflies to make the world colourful,
I sculptured the fluffy clouds to keep the Earth warm,
I created the soil so plants could grow.

My name is Mr Tom David Atkinson,
I am the boy who made it rain to make the sea,
I invented the trees so birds could dwell,
I supplied beaks so birds could sing,
I let oak trees grow so they could be king of the forest,
I did it for you!

Tom Atkinson (10)
Shavington Primary School, Crewe

Beginnings

My name is Amy Louise Howes,
I am the girl who crafted the world.
I painted the rainbow with beautiful colours,
I made the sky for you to look at.
I created the seasons so you can have a change in your life.
I invented butterflies, they give the world colour.
I made the sun set, so it would give
The moon and stars a chance to come out.

My name is Miss Amy Louise Howes,
I am the girl who created the world.
I created the grass to keep the soil underneath warm.
I designed the sea for somewhere for the fish to live.
I created the stars to shine so bright
And I fashioned humans to look after the world for me.
I made the world to give you happiness your whole life through.

Amy Howes (10)
Shavington Primary School, Crewe

Love

I am as young as the sky, but as old as the moon.
I was born in the heart of people sitting by the sunset.
My sister is Happiness and my brother is Joy.
I am wrapped in the warmth of love covered by a veil of hearts.
I live in the heavens of good, where peace is alive.
My greatest fear is to be alone in the pits of Hell.
My greatest success is making love possible between people.

Rebecca Fearnley (10)
Shavington Primary School, Crewe

In This World

My name is Daniel Lloyd Phillips,
I am the boy who fashioned the plants and the creatures
To dwell in the world together.
I am the boy who sculptured the sky
For birds and bees to live in and fly.
I am the boy who crafted humans,
To use all of the space that I gave them.
I am the boy who moulded the world
For everything I created to live in.

My name is Daniel Lloyd Phillips,
I am the boy who crafted the sun
To keep all of the humans warm.
I am the boy who sculptured the planets
To fill up the empty universe.
I am the boy who crafted the world
For all of the creatures to live in,
And I made it all just for you!

Lloyd Phillips (10)
Shavington Primary School, Crewe

Cities

Fumes and pollution all around,
solid concrete on the ground.
Buildings high and buildings low,
as night falls, oh how they glow.

Hundreds of people bustling about,
above the noise they have to shout.
Living in the city can be fun,
so why do people look so glum?

Rebecca Prince (10)
Shavington Primary School, Crewe

Loneliness

I am as old as when the first person was born,
I was born in a cage with nothing to do
and no one to see.
I have two brothers called Anger and Hatred,
I wear a drape of black, of black cloth,
covering all of me.
I live where there is no one to see and
no one to talk to.
My greatest ambition is to make people
see nothing and to make everyone
have nothing to do.
My greatest fear is to not be able to
take people's things away.

Glenn Muirhead (11)
Shavington Primary School, Crewe

If I Had Wings

If I had wings, I would distract the night sky
And the morning sky would creep in.

If I had wings, I would bite the moon
As cold as ice on an ice mountain.

If I had wings, I would go to the heavens
And look down on the Earth where people are clinging.

If I had wings, I would go to the tallest building
And watch people scurry around like ants.

If I had wings, I would watch people,
Like a hawk looking for its prey.

Jamie Flynn (11)
Woodfield Primary School, Chester

If I Had Wings

If I had wings,
> I would fly and touch the sky,
> and then taste the sun.

If I had wings,
> I would touch the sheep on high blue,
> then I would fly and touch the sun.

If I had wings,
> I would fly in and out of clouds like an airplane,
> and swim through the breeze in the sky.

If I had wings,
> I would soar along deserts
> and over hills.

If I had wings,
> I would let the wind push me,
> then go down to the sea.

Georgia Bailiff (11)
Woodfield Primary School, Chester

Confusion

What came first, the chicken or the egg?
Who invented the alphabet?
Why is the world round?
Why are there so many languages in the world?

Confusion is so confusing.

Confusion is purple,
It smells like Stilton cheese.
It tastes of cold spaghetti.
It looks like a wonky question mark.
Confusion feels like you're lost.

Mia Gatward (11)
Woodfield Primary School, Chester

Wings

If I had wings,
    I would glide the wind's breath
        And skim the seven seas.

If I had wings,
    I would sit on the moon
        And fly as softly as a cloud.

If I had wings,
    I would watch the people down below
        And see them go on with their day.

If I had wings,
    I would dream of riding the white horses
        Of the sea and fly the desert.

If I had wings,
    I would fly to Heaven
        And talk to the angels.

If I had wings,
    I would do anything.

Ben Pace (10)
Woodfield Primary School, Chester

Tsunami

A disaster bringer,
A life killer,
A country flooder,
A wave wearer,
A powerful force,
A rushing wave,
A rumbling underground,
A quake and a quiver.
That makes me a tsunami.

Ryan Smith (11)
Woodfield Primary School, Chester

If I Had Wings

If I had wings, I would eat
The planet Mars to the last crumb.

If I had wings, I would taste the
Mountain of snow to the last snowflake.

If I had wings, I would take
A breath of the seven seas.

If I had wings, I would take a
Bit of the best song in the world.

If I had wings, I would
Fly higher than the black hole.

William Gunning (11)
Woodfield Primary School, Chester

Beware Of The Cat

A patterned mat, a furry hat,
A deadly creature, a scary feature,
A nicer rat, a growling bat,
Bed found tread, when not fed,
Fumes rage, gets chucked in cage,
'Pain is over,' says the owner.

Evan McKinney (10)
Woodfield Primary School, Chester

Wings

If I had wings, I would
    rest on the soft clouds
        and float all the way to sea.

If I had wings, I would
    glide through the air
        while scraping the sky.

If I had wings, I would
    go up to the sun when it's cold
        and be warm as water.

If I had wings, I would
    fly to the tallest tree,
        as big as a giant.

If I had wings, I would
    go to the moon at night
        and watch the stars go by.

Alice Ankers (10)
Woodfield Primary School, Chester

A Hard Biter

A hard biter,
A tough flighter

A disaster maker
A high staker

A good waker
A tough shaker

I rhyme with cake,
To make me a snake.

Dale Williams (11)
Woodfield Primary School, Chester

Wings

If I had wings,
>I would dream of walking the river
>and swimming the desert.

If I had wings,
>I would taste a piece of the moon,
>cold and icy as ice cream.

If I had wings,
>I would lie on the soft clouds
>and flow out to sea.

If I had wings,
>I would go up to the dusty and dark sky
>and snap off a piece of star, as bright as gold.

If I had wings
>I would gaze at the plants,
>how they cling to the earth.

Hasna Begum Ali (11)
Woodfield Primary School, Chester

If I Had Wings

If I had wings,
>I would swim through the clouds and glide on the wind's feather.

If I had wings,
>I would taste a chunk of moon as cheesy as a cheese string.

If I had wings,
>I would breathe deep and calm of the trees' oxygen.

If I had wings,
>I would gaze at the people as small as dots.

If I had wings,
>I would swim the seven seas and fly as fast as lightning.

Sabir Kader (10)
Woodfield Primary School, Chester

Wings

If I had wings, I would
Glide over all the skyscrapers in the world
And shine in front of the faces.

If I had wings, I would
Dream of going around the world in eighty days,
But cut the sky in half.

If I had wings, I would
Eat the sky and outrun the police.

If I had wings, I would
Steal the stars and show them to the white horses.

If I had wings, I would
Fly in space with the stampede of stars.

Floyd Williams (10)
Woodfield Primary School, Chester

Vulture

A high lingerer,
A sky scavenger,
A silent sneaker,
A meal grabber,
A carcass creeper,
A patient waiter,
A crafty collector,
A desert demon,
A weird culture,
It's a vulture.

George Welsh (10)
Woodfield Primary School, Chester

Judgement Day

J udgement day is upon us,
U nder the red sky,
D isaster or warming could happen,
G lobal countries could be burned,
E xtinction around every corner,
M elting ice caps raise the sea level,
E xtending rivers, seas and lakes.
N ight brings asteroids,
T omorrow we hope it's better.

D ays will go down in the world to shadow,
A gain we run in fear,
Y esterday we were happy, but today we're not.

Lewis Whitehouse (11)
Woodfield Primary School, Chester

Earthquake

Everything was peaceful,
Then everything went dreadful
When the wave came closer.

Everyone went mad.
They gathered their families,
But some didn't survive.
Their lives have been broken forever,
And can't be fixed.

Abbie Hallmark (10)
Woodfield Primary School, Chester

Earthquake

I hear the sorrow, I hear the cries,
I hear the people saying goodbyes.
I watch the tears fall from the faces,
I see the people hide in different places.
The buildings that were there now have gone.
The schools, the hospitals, now there's only one.
I drink the water with a disgusted face,
This is not the way it's meant to taste.
The people search for survival,
To try and restart their life.
The world was destroyed by the great disaster,
The world will never experience a happy ever after.

Jennifer Plank (11)
Woodfield Primary School, Chester

Tsunami

A boat carrier
A hard barrier

A good eater
A fast cheetah

A water disaster
A still getting faster

A dark cave
A horrible wave.

Andrew Leigh (11)
Woodfield Primary School, Chester